"We've all heard the stereotypes— atheists or that all Christians rejec *actually* think and feel about scien class research in this area sheds light on the views o people of faith."

—**Deborah Haarsma**, astronomer; president of BioLogos

"In her excellent and insightful book, Ecklund brings a desperately needed breath of grace-filled air to the suffocating and suspicious atmosphere polluting many faith communities and many science communities. In an increasingly polarized culture, few things are more important than building epistemic bridges of humility, respect, and curiosity. I wish every one of my parishioners would read this book."

—**Tom Nelson**, senior pastor, Christ Community Church; president, Made to Flourish

"The contemporary church is fighting against so much today, and in the process we are losing one of the most profound gifts the church uniquely offers the world: community. In chapter 4, an interview subject named Jill had been told that her own unique gifts of wonder and curiosity were not valued. In reality they are desperately needed; without these gifts the Christian world struggles to grasp the transformational beauty that is the mystery of the kingdom of God. A thoughtful and spirited treatise."

—**Juanita Rasmus**, senior pastor, St. John's Church, Houston, Texas; author of *Learning to Be*

"Through the lens of sociological data and personal experience, Ecklund paints a thought-provoking and compelling picture of how both science and Christian faith, properly understood, help drive out fear of the unknown and cultivate shared virtues, including humility, intellectual curiosity, and even doubt. Ecklund's voice is refreshingly honest."

—**Praveen Sethupathy**, Center for Vertebrate Genomics, Cornell University

"Ecklund helps us see how faith and science are not opposing forces. When understood and embraced, they can in fact reinforce and strengthen one's faith and scholarship. Ecklund's contagious hope for the people of God to see the breadth and depth of God's glory made plain to us through the marvels of science is inspiring."

—**Korie Edwards**, Ohio State University

Other Books by Elaine Howard Ecklund

Secularity and Science: What Scientists around the World Really Think about Religion

Religion vs. Science: What Religious People Really Think

Science vs. Religion: What Scientists Really Think

Korean American Evangelicals: New Models for Civic Life

WHY SCIENCE *and* FAITH NEED EACH OTHER

EIGHT SHARED VALUES THAT MOVE US BEYOND FEAR

ELAINE HOWARD ECKLUND

BrazosPress
a division of Baker Publishing Group
Grand Rapids, Michigan

Published by Brazos Press
a division of Baker Publishing Group
PO Box 6287, Grand Rapids, MI 49516-6287
www.brazospress.com

Printed in the United States of America

Library of Congress Cataloging-in-Publication Data
Names: Ecklund, Elaine Howard, author.
Title: Why science and faith need each other : eight shared values that move us beyond fear / Elaine Howard Ecklund.
Description: Grand Rapids, Michigan : Brazos Press, a division of Baker Publishing Group, 2020. | Includes bibliographical references.
Identifiers: LCCN 2019039128 | ISBN 9781587434365 (paperback)
Subjects: LCSH: Religion and science. | Christianity.
Classification: LCC BL240.3 .E26 2020 | DDC 201/.65—dc23
LC record available at https://lccn.loc.gov/2019039128

ISBN 978-1-58743-488-4 (casebound)

The author is represented by the literary agency of Creative Trust Literary Group, LLC.

20 21 22 23 24 25 26 7 6 5 4 3 2 1

To Karl and Anika

To Teresa (1955–2019)

Contents

Acknowledgments

THE EXPERIENCE of writing this book has left me profoundly grateful for my communities. Thank you, in particular, to Hayley Hemstreet and Laura Achenbaum; to Deidra Coleman and Robert A. Thomson Jr.; to Dan Bolger and Sharan Kaur Mehta; to Rose Kantorczyk and Shannon Klein; and especially to Michael McDowell and Rachel Schneider Vlachos for their help with research for the book. I am grateful to the advisory board members for this project: Harvey Clemons, Greg Cootsona, Daniel Espinoza, Deborah Haarsma, Se Kim, Richard J. Mouw, Wayne Park, and Steve Wells. Thank you to Jeff Smith and to members of our Science in Congregations team at St. Andrews, with whom I discussed the ideas in this book often, and thanks especially to the late Teresa Phillips, who embodied them. I am grateful for Heather Wax's editing and the guidance she provided. Special thanks to my agent, Kathryn Helmers, for initially believing in the idea for this book. Special thanks to my editor, Katelyn Beaty; to Melisa Blok; and to everyone at Brazos Press. I am most grateful for the support of my family and especially for my husband, Karl, and my daughter, Anika, who give me all my best stories.

This publication was made possible through the support of a grant from Templeton Religion Trust ("Reaching Evangelical American Leaders to Change Hearts and Minds," TRT0191, Elaine Howard Ecklund PI). The opinions expressed in this publication are those of the author and do not necessarily reflect the views of Templeton Religion Trust or Rice University.

PART 1

BUILDING BLOCKS

1

From Fear to Understanding

"The game is over. Come out now!" Anika yells to her friend. "Come out now, or my mom will give you a spanking!" There is no truth behind her threat, yet my eight-year-old daughter delivers it with incredible conviction. It has its origin in an incident that occurred several years earlier.

Anika was three years old and I was picking her up from day care. That day, I was tired from work and parenting solo while my husband was away. I parked, found Anika, and started to slowly lead her to the car. She begged to stay a few more minutes to play with her friends. I acquiesced.

They started a game of hide-and-seek, and I turned away for a minute to talk with another parent. Daylight was starting to fade, and I expected that at any moment Anika would sidle up to me and wrap her arms around my leg. After a few minutes, when that hadn't happened, I started to look around. "Anika, it's time to go," I called out. No response. One by one, the parents and children got into their cars and drove away. I called again, "Anika, I really mean it; it's time to go!" Still nothing. I picked up my bag and walked over to where she and her friends had been playing, but I did not see anyone. "Anika! Where are you?" I said, this time louder and with more urgency. A friend left her child buckled in the car and came to help me look. We did not see any movement near the bushes where the children had been playing. Full-fledged anxiety had set in and my heart was beating more quickly. The day care's associate director assured me she hadn't seen any children come inside the building. I kept yelling out as my heart rate continued to rise. "Anika, Anika! Where are you?!" I was now panicking. There were no sounds except my own voice.

I checked up and down the street, opening the doors of parked cars to look inside. "Ma'am, are you trying to break into my car?" I heard a man ask, not particularly angry but very perplexed. I did not answer him. I had a singular mission. With tears streaming down my face, I commissioned this stranger in the search. The associate director checked inside the center and around its perimeter, then activated the safety protocol for a missing child. If we did not find Anika in five minutes, she would call the police.

In that moment, I truly believed that I might not find her. I felt fear like I never had before, and my fear motivated my actions. The mother who stayed behind to help took her son out of his car seat, and they checked a side street. "Anika, where are you?!" I yelled at full capacity. I did not hear what anyone said, and I did not care what anyone thought.

Suddenly, I felt a familiar touch on my right leg, and then I heard, "Mommy, will I have my TV taken away tonight?" I grabbed her and hugged her so tight that she asked me to loosen my grip. Even now, nearly five years later, my heart races as I write this.

It was the little boy who found her. After he was released from his car seat, he walked over to some bushes by the day care center; he told us he had heard her breathing and her giggle as he came near. The entire time I was searching, Anika had been hiding within ten feet of me. She had heard me. She had heard the associate director. She had heard my friend and the others helping in the search. She had heard all of us calling to her, and yet she had chosen not to answer.

I let her down softly onto the sidewalk, then grabbed her arm again, looked into her face, and, again not caring what others thought, yelled, “I am so angry. I want to give you such a spanking!” She started sobbing, and the little boy who found her started sobbing too. “Let’s take a step back,” the associate director of the day care said as she gently touched my arm. “There is a fine line between fear and anger.” I do not spank Anika, and I did not then, but my fear—so palpable just minutes before when I would have done literally anything to find her—had transitioned to anger, and the emotion took over. It made me rash and impulsive, unable to think clearly and wisely.

For a long time after that day, fear was at the center of my relationship with Anika. It wasn’t just a feeling; it turned into a way of being, a kind of physical and emotional practice. I was constantly turning my head so that I could keep her in view; my heart would race if she left my sight for more than a minute. I wanted to touch her or hold her hand at all times, just to make sure I knew where she was and knew she couldn’t get away. Having her on such a short leash led to conflict and stifled her sense of curiosity about the world.

Over time, I did become less afraid, however, and my relationship with her has changed. She has grown and become wiser about boundaries, and I have learned to let her explore and be curious, to venture off a bit, believing she will still come back to me. I no longer need to turn my head to see her all the time. Little by little, more and more, I rely on trust, prudence, and courage. I would not have wished for the experience of thinking I had lost her, but it did teach me something about myself: when I feel anger, the more true emotion is often fear. So now I ask, "What am I afraid of?"

Quelling Anger and Recognizing Fear

I bring this lesson to my academic work on how Christians view science and the relationship between religion and science. Fear can masquerade as anger, leading to conflict, so when we see conflict between religious belief and science, we should examine whether there might be underlying fear and try to understand it. Is there fear that science might contradict or diminish elements of faith? Fear that accepting certain scientific ideas will decrease the strength of faith or lead away from faith altogether? Fear about certain scientific findings and technologies that raise contentious ethical and theological questions? If Christians are responding to science based on such fear, how might we assuage it or replace the emotion with more productive habits or practices?[1]

Sociologists like me are interested in group behaviors. We are interested in how groups have an impact on individuals and how groups can bring changes to society, for good and for bad. One way we study this is by listening to people's life stories and analyzing to what extent these individual stories represent the groups that these individuals are part of. And we understand our own story best when we compare it with the stories of others. Social-scientific research and data also allow us to get past the loud, combative voices that often drive public debate and allow us to gain a more nuanced and accurate picture of what people think, value, and believe. Sociology helps us understand which group practices work best for accomplishing particular aims.[2] Sociology does not have the same tools as philosophy or theology; it cannot tell us the right way to live. But if we know *how* we want our communities or churches to be different, then sociology can help us change group cultures and engage in practices that help us effect these changes.

My Studies

For the past fifteen years, I have been studying what religious believers think about science and what scientists think about religion.[3] In total, I have surveyed nearly 41,000 religious believers and scientists (both believers and non-believers) on the relationship between religion and science. I have also conducted 1,290 in-depth, face-to-face interviews with religious people and with scientists, including religious scientists. I became interested in this topic because of how both faith and science have marked my own life and because I think science and faith address the biggest and most important questions of life. Research shows that the views people hold about the relationship between religion and science are important. They can influence whom people vote for and, by extension, public financial support for scientific research. Views on the relationship between religion and science can also influence whether an individual goes to church and whether young people stay in church. Research finds that many youth are leaving the church because they perceive irreconcilable conflict between Christianity and science.[4]

In the churches I have visited, I have met Christians who keep their children out of certain science classes, afraid that scientific education will lead them to doubt, and ultimately reject, their faith. When helping their children choose colleges and universities, some Christian parents worry about what scientists who teach at those schools will say about faith. Black and Latino/a Christians sometimes worry about being part of science and technology fields where they are underrepresented not only in race and ethnicity but also in faith. Christian women and girls who want to pursue scientific careers wonder if they will be marginalized in their Christian communities for their scientific aspirations and marginalized in the scientific community for both their gender and their faith. Some Christians worry about certain medical technologies and research, whether they are ethical and whether they take into account the uniqueness of the human being and what it means to be made in the image of God. I have met many Christians who are afraid of how science will impact their faith and how scientists will influence religion and its place in society. I have also met many Christians who want to have more productive conversations about the relationship between science and religion and ways to better engage with science and the technologies that, at times, seem to be taking over our society.

One of my biggest research projects was a major study on the relationship between faith and science that focused on evangelicals in the US, conducted in partnership with the American Association for the Advancement of Science's Dialogue on Science, the Ethics and Religion Program, and the National Association of Evangelicals. My research revealed that while Christians are different from other religious groups in how they view science, evangelical Christians are a special case. While there are many ways to define what it means to be an evangelical Christian, in this book I am drawing from the work of fellow social scientists to define evangelicals as Christians who hold to an authoritative reading of the Bible and accept the Bible as divinely inspired.[5] Evangelical Christians also believe in the literal resurrection of Jesus from the dead. I have found through my studies that evangelical Christians are more likely than members of other religious groups to perceive tensions between their faith and science. They are also more likely than those from other religions to be suspicious of the scientific community and to consult their pastors about difficult scientific issues.[6] They are more likely to perceive tensions between faith and science. Thus, it is important to pay particular attention to how evangelical Christians feel about science.[7]

Behind This Book

For this book, I analyzed pieces of my data that were particularly relevant to Christian communities and collected new data from Christian scientists at the top of their fields who are also involved in church communities. I also conducted interviews with a large and diverse group of Christians from across the country. I examined what influences their attitudes toward science and the differences in their individual beliefs. I uncovered the scientific issues where their faith has the strongest impact. I wanted to understand what they actually think about the relationship between religion and science, and why.

The content of this book is rooted in social science research, and it is filled with the stories of Christians and scientists who share their experiences with integrating science and faith. Some have reconciled science and religion as systems of ideas. Others have reconciled science and religion in a more personal way. You will hear from those who are both scientists and Christians and who have found ways to communicate or relate to other scientists. (The individuals I quote here from my research studies are meant to represent the views of groups they are part of.) For example, you will hear from scientists who are people of faith or work with religious colleagues and who accept the idea that Christian faith can be reconciled with science. These folks act differently from others when controversial issues related to science and faith arise. They are exemplars I want you to meet.[8]

I have designed this book especially for my own faith community: committed Christians—especially those who are part of a church—and the pastors who lead them. I hope that learning from hundreds of believers around the country who have shared their views on science and religion will provide you with new ways of thinking about scientific issues and the relationship between faith and science. If you are a congregant, this book will show you how a broad range of fellow Christians approach scientific topics and will introduce you to Christian scientists and non-scientists who have reconciled science and religious beliefs in ways that grow their faith. I hope it will also help you develop practices for engaging productively with the relationship between science and religion in your own life. If you are a pastor, this book can be a resource for including discussions of science in congregational life, sermons, or classes and for generally helping those in your church develop better practices for engaging with science.

When I started writing this book, I searched my house for a notebook from a class I took more than twenty years ago as an undergraduate at Cornell University. In that class, taught by Norman Kretzmann on the philosopher Thomas Aquinas, I began to think deeply about the Christian virtues, which Aquinas saw as practices or habits that tend toward the good. In studying, interviewing, and working with both Christians and scientists, it struck me that they seemed to share many of the same virtues. When Robert Pennock, a philosopher at Michigan State University in East Lansing, surveyed scientists in the US "about the importance of various virtues for the exemplary practice of science and how they are transmitted in the scientific community," he found that scientists believed science should be based on a set of values that included curiosity, honesty, and humility.[9] These are indeed some of the same virtues I have seen promoted and cultivated in faith communities around the country, including my own.

Are there other shared virtues between science and religion, I began to wonder, that could help unite the two realms? Could a set of shared virtues make it easier for Christians to communicate with scientists and accept and engage with the ideas, findings, and processes of science? While we Christians see all virtues as ultimately coming from God, are certain virtues better honed in Christian communities and other virtues better honed in scientific communities? Do Christian scientists bring religious virtues to their scientific communities, and can they bring scientific virtues to their religious communities? I believe the core virtues that guide the practice and habits of science and religion are more similar than we think; yet there are also some key differences. I am proposing a new approach to discussing the relationship between science and faith: I see science and faith not just as sets of ideas but as groups of people, and I am convinced that scientists and Christians share common virtues that, if brought to light, will lead to common ground. I am also convinced that by recognizing the common virtues between our faith and science, and where our values differ, we Christians can begin to develop a more effective and meaningful relationship with science and scientists.

The first three chapters of this book tell us about the building blocks of virtues—how virtues are birthed in our communities and are part of what it means to be human. Starting with chapter 4, this book explores eight key virtues of Christianity—curiosity, doubt, humility, creativity, healing, awe, shalom, and gratitude—and how these virtues are practiced in the scientific community. The virtues of curiosity, doubt, humility, and creativity are crucial to the scientific process and, I argue, ought to be a core part of Christian communities. The virtues of healing, awe, shalom, and gratitude reveal how science and faith come together in redemptive practices.

This book aims to show Christians the values they share with scientists, how Christian scientists see religious values in their scientific work, and how Christian communities might draw on the virtues they share with the scientific community to better connect with science and scientists. At the end of each chapter, I'll provide questions that both lay Christians and pastors can use to continue the discussion.

As the Bible tells us, "There is no fear in love. But perfect love drives out fear" (1 John 4:18). Fear doesn't have to lead to anger and alienation. We can take a step back, respond less rashly, think more clearly and wisely, and work to improve the relationship we have with science. I believe that Christians can develop a new and enriched love for science through a new approach that focuses on the virtues that scientific and Christian communities have in common.

Further Discussion

1. Talk together about practices your church has for engaging topics related to faith and science. What does your pastor or another church leader say during sermons about faith and science?
2. What topics related to science and faith are discussed in Sunday school classes or other educational venues?
3. If science is not discussed at all in your church, why not?
4. Discuss science and faith in relationship to fear. What kinds of fears does science raise, if it raises any?

2

Overlapping Communities

JAMES IS A PLASMA SCIENTIST and an evangelical Christian who believes his work affirms his faith and vice versa. When we met, he talked about his scientific work as a spiritual calling, and he believes his spirituality has encouraged him to continue this work. He says, "I need science, from my perspective as a scientist, to then make me understand that the scientifically impossible makes Jesus Christ's resurrection so extraordinary and substantiates his claim that he is the Son of God and that he died for our sins and is resurrected just as we have hope in the resurrection."[1]

James says his coworkers seem accepting of his faith. "I have a poster on my office wall that says, 'Slow me down, Lord,' things like that, and sometimes I get kidded about the fact that sometimes I should read the poster on my wall when I work too hard," he says, laughing. James also considers himself fortunate to have attended churches where his scientific work has not been an issue with leaders or congregants. He recounts several instances of his pastor speaking about the relationship between science and faith from the pulpit, and even inviting him and other scientists in the congregation to serve on panel discussions in Sunday school classes or at other churches. James addresses his scientific work directly in his discussions with other congregants and says they have been very receptive to this dialogue.

James is part of two different communities: a community of scientists and a community of Christians. Talking with him reminded me that attitudes toward science and faith are established, separately and differently, within these communities—and these attitudes in turn have an impact on the relationship between the two communities. Core virtues are also established within these communities, and we learn the core virtues and values of our communities, and strategies to practice them, from the people around us. We might think of virtues as the glue that holds well-functioning communities together. Scientists who are Christians have the potential to be special because they have developed both scientific virtues and Christian virtues, sometimes recognizing similarities, sometimes feeling tension, and sometimes bringing the virtues of one community to the other.

Christians in Science

Still, many Christian scientists say they feel marginalized in the scientific community. Some I interviewed say they feel scrutinized by colleagues who seem to see faith as a limiting factor for scientific understanding. Some also report feeling uncomfortable in their workplace due to the negative attitudes and stereotypes they feel some colleagues hold toward faith and people of faith.

When I conducted a study of US scientists who work outside of universities in research and development, I found that evangelical scientists were much more likely than other evangelicals to believe scientists are hostile toward religion.[2] Many evangelical scientists believe that nonreligious scientists are suspicious of them because some scientists think that evangelical faith—even more than other forms of Christian faith—has the potential to compromise scientific work and rigor. My interviews with nonreligious scientists support this view. A graduate student in biology, for example, described an evangelical Christian colleague as

> all about God all the time, and Jesus; all Jesus all the time. She is very vocal about it and often she will say how God is great or like, "Thank you, Jesus," for like doing blah, blah, blah thing. . . . [Scientists who are Christians] are very quiet because they know their colleagues either will ridicule them or will question their scientific work and their objectivity, . . . but I definitely see that there's a conflict in how she's able to understand things. Her work is good for what it is, but it's never going to get past some level of reflection because of [her faith].[3]

In my experience studying scientists' attitudes toward religion, it is extremely uncommon for a Christian scientist to talk this much about faith in the scientific workplace. But what *is* typical is for nonreligious scientists to feel like the faith of evangelical Christian scientists *might* compromise their scientific work. And conversations like the one with the scientist above simply confirm such stereotypes.

For example, one evangelical professor of physics said, "I do find that it is extremely common to be in casual conversation with my professional colleagues and they say incredibly ignorant and stereotyping things about people of faith."[4] A scientist who works in genetics said he has encountered the perception that Christians in science are foremost trying to spread their faith as opposed to focusing on their studies, and in his perception, some non-Christian scientists view evangelical scientists in particular as using their positions in the scientific community to "dismantle secular ideas from within the vanguard of academia."[5] Other scientists who are Christians say that such attitudes might exist because scientists who are not religious "have just never encountered a Christian that can make sense to them and that they trust."[6] Because nonreligious scientists do not personally know a large group of evangelicals who are scientists—or even those evangelical Christians who are friendly to scientific ideas—such stereotypes continue.

The findings from one of my studies show that a sizeable minority of US evangelical scientists—about 32 percent—have perceived religious discrimination in the workplace.[7] This is a good deal higher than the 21 percent of evangelical non-scientists who reported religious discrimination in the workplace. My survey of academic scientists also revealed that Protestant and Muslim scientists in the US are more likely than other US scientists to feel they have experienced religious discrimination in the workplace;[8] in fact, 40 percent of Protestant scientists in the US say they have experienced some degree of religious discrimination in the workplace. Among Muslim scientists, the share was even higher at 57 percent. For comparison, only 11 percent of non-Protestant and non-Muslim scientists reported the same. My colleague Chris Scheitle and I found that, among physicists, the higher rate of religious discrimination experienced by Protestants and Muslims is related to their higher levels of religious practice. In biology, however, where the tensions between science and religion have been more public and prominent—around topics such as evolution and human embryonic stem cell research—we found that "simply identifying with certain religious traditions might violate the professional norm and move a biologist from 'us' to 'them.'"[9]

I have also met evangelical and non-evangelical Christian scientists who say they have *not* experienced overt discrimination as Christians working in science, and yet they feel their colleagues treat or look at them somewhat differently due to their faith. As one scientist told me, "There are some people here who view my Christian faith as a curiosity, maybe an oddity, hard to say."[10]

Like James, several Christian scientists say their faith does not often come up at work. A number of Christian scientists say that many of their colleagues continue to be completely unaware or surprised that some of their colleagues are religious. An evangelical professor of physics told me, "It's amazing the degree to which I think the vast majority of professional scientists do not realize that they actually do know some people who are people of deep religious faith."[11]

Some Christian scientists are pleasantly surprised at how nonreligious scientists react to their faith when it's discovered, leading these Christian scientists to re-examine perceptions they have of how the scientific community judges faith. "I've been surprised at how gracious people can be," says Sarah, a biology researcher, "and I think I have to take a lot of my own medicine, where I tell religious folks that scientists aren't out to get them."[12] When Christian scientists discover that not all of their nonreligious science colleagues are hostile to people of faith, then they may begin to talk more about their faith.

Scientists in Church Communities

Research shows that trust in science has steadily declined over the past thirty years among people who regularly attend church,[13] yet I have found in my research that Christians in the US tend to be more skeptical of *scientists* than of science itself. Christians often talk to me about being more worried about the agenda and aims of scientists than about the implications of scientific findings. According to one scientist I interviewed, people in churches sometimes expect that scientists "browbeat Christians with science. Then that makes Christians understandably upset, and then [Christians] themselves begin to equate science as being something that is at the heart of disproving their faith."[14]

One evangelical scientist who teaches at an Ivy League school speaks of a "rich history of partnership between science and faith that often goes ignored." He said that "it's more *scientists* and *people of faith*" who are at odds. He explained, "I think there is a fear there that perhaps there's an agenda or an attempt to kind of marginalize people of faith, and I think there are things that have happened in our history . . . that have brought us to this point where there's this pretty deep chasm that separates us."[15]

Some Christians feel that scientists specifically aim to disprove Christianity through science. One evangelical Christian woman I interviewed said, "I think that [scientists] would be more apt to find a bone in the ground and say this is the missing link, this is what proves evolution, we can finally shut up those rotten Christians."[16] I have met Christian parents who worry their children will encounter scientists who will discourage their faith, and in one of my surveys, 25 percent of evangelical Christians said they place "hardly any" confidence in general in colleges and universities.[17]

Sarah, a biologist who studies evolution and climate change, grew up in a faith community that told her she had to choose between being a Christian and being a scientist.[18] While she was undeterred from pursuing science, she suspects that others in her church were led to believe that being a scientist was not a possible path for a committed Christian, especially a Christian woman. She said many of her fellow believers view her as an anomaly and find it hard to fathom how she reconciles her work and her faith. A Christian professor of physics similarly told me in a sort of resigned way, "I have never experienced support for being a scientist at church, but then again, I don't think at most churches that anyone really experiences support for their scientific work."[19]

I have met some scientists, however, who *do* feel a more collaborative relationship between faith and science within their churches. Many scientists who felt their church supported their scientific work offered possible reasons for this attitude, such as church size, congregational makeup, and an environment that encouraged questioning and discussion. One biologist I interviewed told me he feels valued in his church and that its leaders appreciate hearing his perspective. "I tend to be deployed as the 'science guy' here," he said, "which is to say when somebody needs a talk on science and Christian faith, whether it's a student [in a campus] ministry or Sunday school session, . . . they will ask me, 'Will you give a talk on this?'"[20] A professor of medicine similarly described how his fellow congregants value his scientific work and perspective. When they learn he is a scientist, they "actually really embrace it. They're actually heartened by it, and they're interested, and . . . they're like, 'Oh, you're a doctor and you're a believer, you do science and you believe that? That's really cool. . . . Tell me more about what you do.'"[21]

Jaime, an evolutionary biologist, grew up in a church with positive attitudes toward science. "My impression of pastors and Sunday school teachers was that their view was that there were a lot of ways to glorify God," she said, "and understanding the world [as a scientist] was a way to glorify God." Her current church is "very supportive" of her scientific work and has come to view her as an expert and resource, asking her to lead Sunday school classes and youth classes for congregants in order to explain scientific topics and dispel stereotypes. To be encouraged in this way in her church is extraordinary, she said, and a bit unusual compared with other churches she has attended. She is not quite sure what motivates her specific faith community to want to learn more, yet she recalls one occasion in which her pastor asked her to lead a Sunday school class on evolution. "The parents of the confirmation students were feeling very stressed out that their children were being told in school that evolution was problematic for religious people," she remembered. "And so these . . . thirteen- and fourteen-year-old people were buying into their school's perspective that if they want to be a scientist, . . . they might find religious faith more challenging."[22]

Other Christian scientists told me they believe their church community could be supportive, but they do not yet feel comfortable discussing their scientific work in their church. A professor of chemistry told me, "There was sometimes in the church the idea that children needed to be protected from the university, not only because of science but in part because of scientists." She found this ironic because she was present when people in her church were talking about their fear of scientists. She went on: "And here I was a scientist sitting next to my ten-year-old daughter in the church, a professor at that very university [they were referring to]."[23]

A professor of medicine who works with children with a rare form of cancer said he has a lot of things he is struggling with in his scientific work. And he feels like he should be talking to his pastor, but he doesn't quite know how to get the conversation going:

> I do feel like I could go to him and say, "Hey I'm really wrestling with this." . . . Maybe I should be more vulnerable because I don't really seek his counsel for things like this [chuckles]. . . . I guess there's somewhat of a separation there [between scientific work and church life]. . . . I'm not necessarily looking to spiritual leaders to help me make those hard decisions [about treating children or what kind of science I should do next]. I am instead looking to colleagues and, you know, science.[24]

A Christian biologist told me,

> We just are in the middle of wrapping up a four-week adult education series on science and Christian faith, and [I am going to

> be] interviewed as part of that class. So, you know, overall I feel pretty valued, but . . . I would echo what [I've heard] . . . a lot of Christians in science say about their life in church, and that is that they do feel a bit lonely in the sense that maybe they don't have opportunities to think out loud about Christian faith and their professional science or to share the fruits of what they're doing with people in the congregation very often.[25]

These quotations underscore that many of the Christian scientists I have interviewed over the years practice a "secret science" where they just do not talk about their scientific work at church. In part, this is because no one invites them to talk about it. Because of their secret science, churchgoers can continue to believe that no one at church is a scientist. In reality, the best interlocutors for the science-and-faith conversation might be the scientists sitting right in the pews.

Collaboration and Community

When I surveyed adults in the US about science and religion, 14 percent said they view science and religion as in conflict, and they are on the side of religion. This means that if they perceive a disagreement between religion and science, they will favor the teachings of their faith. Among evangelicals, that number rises to 25 percent. The more surprising finding, however, is that many evangelical Christians do not believe science and religion are necessarily in conflict. My surveys show that they *are more likely* than the general population to think that science and religion can collaborate. Among US adults overall, 38 percent believe science and religion can be used to support each other and that collaboration between the two realms would be possible and beneficial. Among evangelical Christians, the number goes up to 46 percent. Evangelical *scientists* are even more likely to believe in collaboration between science and religion: nearly 60 percent express support for collaboration between the two realms. When I surveyed scientists who work outside universities, I found that in general more scientists believed that the relationship between science and religion is one of collaboration than that science and religion are in conflict or completely independent.[26]

One scientist in immunology I spoke with told me he felt science and faith could fill gaps the other may leave or provide possible solutions for questions the other cannot answer. "There are certainly areas where religion, . . . or spirituality, or Scripture, has not been able to shine light on understanding, you know, on what the underlying answer is," he said, but "every scientific field, mathematical equation, breaks down at some point."[27]

Another scientist said, "Being a scientist helped me to think hard about theology." He worked as a scientist for three decades. He explained, "One of the things that scientists . . . are pretty good at is they have to look at their hypotheses, weigh them against the empirical data they have, and, you know, sometimes their hypotheses don't fully account for the data, and so they have to hold their hypotheses somewhat loosely, and I think that's been of great value to me when I think about my Christian faith and think about theological constructs that Christians like to generate to think about the Christian faith."[28] This scientist had begun to hold both theological and scientific constructs loosely, not to doubt their truth but to humbly expect that his understanding of them was inherently limited. A professor of genetics told me about her work trying to connect the school of genetics with the school of divinity at her university. She has plans to speak with the dean about her goal, which is "to bring science and spirituality together [through the people who teach each]."[29]

One evangelical scientist told me that, in his view, "the church needs basically to drop its fear of science." As he sees it, "Both the church and science are interested in the truth. Now, they are a little bit different aspects of the truth, but I don't think that either side needs to view the other antagonistically. And I understand how science feels because of some of the past oppressions from the church. So maybe there needs to be a little forgiveness . . . on both sides."[30]

As Robert Pennock's study of scientific virtues showed us, those in scientific communities may hold core virtues that are similar to the virtues upheld in many Christian communities, such as curiosity and humility.[31] My own research has uncovered other common virtues between the two communities, including creativity, awe, joy, and gratitude. Both communities strive to heal the world around them. Churches should become a place where Christian scientists can highlight these shared virtues—in adult education classes, sermons, teachings, or other public roles that allow them to share their work and knowledge with those in churches.

Communities are incredibly important. Research has shown time and again that we judge people we perceive as similar to us as more moral, trustworthy, and competent, and we tend to see ourselves as similar to those who are part of our communities or who share our values.[32] Indeed, this research shows that participation in *communities* is really important (and often even necessary) for long-term change to result in individuals.

Research also shows that when people believe a scientific expert shares their values, they can be more likely to accept that expert's conclusions.[33] By focusing on values and virtues that Christians and scientists have in common, scientists who are Christians can act as *boundary pioneers*, helping the members of their faith communities better connect, cooperate, and be in dialogue with members of the scientific community and helping the scientific community better connect with faith communities.

A few years back, my congregation received a grant from the Scientists in Congregations program.[34] It has since run a series of programs in which scientists in the congregation speak about their scientific work and about their perspectives on and struggles with science and faith. The congregation also had well-known scientists from around the world give talks on hot-button science and religion issues, such as the role of God in the origin of the world, creation and evolution, the meaning and the sanctity of life, what it means to be human, and how we can approach the relationship between science and faith.

Initially, the congregation was hesitant. Some were concerned about how the program would be received and how it might affect the faith of church members. Yet the program was a resounding success. "I always thought of my work [as a scientist] as completely separate from my actual faith or something that needed to 'be dealt with,'" a scientist in my church and on our science-in-congregations planning committee told me. "But through presenting my own perspective on the compatibility, for me, between science and Christian faith, I came to see how my work and my Christian faith can be deeply integrated." Both adults and youth enthusiastically and thoughtfully participated in the discussions, and turnout at adult education classes tripled. Even participants who did not agree with the viewpoints being presented remained civil and open to the program, agreeing to disagree and to continue their involvement in the dialogue. One church member said that thinking through divisive issues during the program showed her ways she can "stay in the conversation without walking away" when faced with future debates involving science and religion. She felt the program was particularly meaningful and effective because it utilized the expertise of church members whom other congregants knew and trusted. In other words, even though some of the very best scientists in the world had been invited to participate in the church program, key to the program's success were the scientists actually from within the congregation's own community.

In discussions about science and faith, it is especially important to engage young congregants, who are in the midst of considering their future educational pursuits and careers. A biologist told me that every few years his church has a "science and Christian faith all-day seminar, and . . . we try to have some scientists come and talk about how amazing the natural world is and just to kind of get university students marinating in the joy of discovery."[35] In my own experience of running the Scientists in Congregations program at my church, I found that it is youth who are particularly hungry to hear more about the science and faith interface, to have honest conversations about genuine struggles.

Scientists can participate in churches in many ways. A scientist told me about a talk she gave to her congregation, which she titled "My Life as a Scientist," and explained, "I've done a faith and science integration talk, and my husband and I have also led a Sunday school series where we've looked at the divisive issues over the last sixty years, including climate change, abortion, evolution, dancing (from long ago), [and] women in office."[36] Scientists also talked about leading the worship services and singing for the church so that congregants trusted them as fellow Christians who could still worship God while participating in science. One evangelical scientist talked about a sermon his pastor gave him the opportunity to deliver:

> So this was asking a few of us to stand up and say, well, what is actually your work? . . . It was super cool. And that's one of the reasons I really love him and love his church. And so that was neat, because then I could stand up and talk about some of the cases I've worked with and some of the genetic analyses we've done and some of the papers we've published. And so people were actually very, very interested. And there was definitely no "how can you *do* this as a Christian?" It was very much like, "Oh that's cool, you know, that's really interesting!"[37]

And there are rare occasions when we see scientific and religious communities really engage each other. In an essay in *Physics Today*, physicist Tom McLeish (a committed Christian, who is also a Fellow of the Royal Society, one of the UK's greatest scientific honors) writes about attending a public debate about a controversial scientific issue and witnessing something unique: "This gathering was different. Strongly opposing views were expressed, but their proponents listened to each other. Everyone was keen to grasp both the knowns and the uncertainties of the geological science and technology. Social science and geophysics both drew sustained civil dialog." McLeish goes on about his experience that night: "The notion of different priorities was understood—and some people actually *changed* their views."[38] Only when we engage groups that we think of as "the other" in a genuine way is there the possibility to cross boundaries and change minds.

For some Christians, it may seem odd to think of "scientific" virtues. But values form the foundation of the scientific community and how scientists think about and practice their work, just like they form the basis for how Christians practice their faith. Before we explore these virtues, it is important to examine another building block, the one that gives us the capacity for virtue—our humanness, something that seems at stake for many Christians when they begin to discuss evolution.

Further Discussion

1. What has been the role of the Christian community in your life? How about the scientific community?
2. What kind of virtues are most embodied in your church community?

3. How can your church community address science and faith issues without compromising the cohesion of the community?
4. In your experience, to what extent is your church community suspicious of scientists?
5. Are there scientists in your church? To what extent do you know scientists at your church? How might you get to know them better?

3

Creative Evolution: Moving Past the Origins Debate

"SO THEN, where did I come from?" asked a teenager at a Bible study I was sitting in on as part of my research. As a sociologist studying religion, it was not unusual for me to visit these kinds of meetings and discussion groups. Here, I was conducting research with a professor from nearby Cornell University, a school that pastors and parents in this church hoped some of their youth might attend. Although this rural evangelical church was similar to the church I was raised in, I was now an outsider looking in rather than an insider looking out. In my mid-twenties, I was still young enough to blend in with this group of teenagers and young adults.

"Where did I come from?" the teen asked again, more insistent this time. He would not let up. "What does this mean for me? Where did I come from?" he asked, now a bit frustrated at being ignored. The pastor looked a little stunned, as if he did not want to take on this question, but he returned to his notes about the transition from high school to college and stressed to the group that it was wise to be wary because there would be professors in biology and sociology who would try to teach them things about evolution that would take them away from their faith. (My ears perked up at the mention of my own discipline of sociology being one of the "dangerous" ones!) "And so," he said, "when these professors tell you where you come from, that you come from monkeys, know in your heart that you are not an animal, but that you are special, you are unique, and you are created by God and in his image; you are uniquely human." I could tell that the teen felt a bit deflated.

The first page of the Bible tells us that "God created [humankind] in his own image, in the image of God he created them" (Gen. 1:27). It is a core Christian doctrine that God created the world and that humans were created in the image of God, thus holding a special place in creation. Whether the creation story in Genesis is believed as a literal description or an allegory, it provides Christians with an indelible sense that humans are unique within creation and have a meaningful, God-given purpose for living. We set the stage with a discussion of humanness and evolution because, for many Christians, this God-ordained "humanness" is of the highest value and is the source of all our capacity for virtue.

My interviews with Christians have helped me understand how the idea that humans are made by God in the image of God can influence how Christians approach certain scientific technologies and ideas, particularly the theory of evolution. Some Christians worry about what accepting evolution would mean for core tenets of their faith. Yet my research also shows that many Christians accept evolution while maintaining firm Christian convictions regarding the creator role of God and the uniqueness of humans among other life forms.

What Christians Think about Evolution

Instead of just asking people whether they believe in creationism or evolution, as other researchers had done, I asked Christian respondents to choose from among six explanations for the origin and development of life on earth:

- Young-earth creationism (God created everything within the past ten thousand years)
- Recent human creation in the midst of an old earth (God created the universe and the earth billions of years ago; plants and animals evolved over millions of years from earlier life forms, but God intervened to create humans within the past ten thousand years)
- God-guided evolution (God created the universe and the earth billions of years ago; God started and has guided human evolution over millions of years)
- Intelligent design (the universe and earth came into being billions of years ago, and humans evolved over millions of years according to the design of an intelligent force)
- God-initiated evolution (God created the universe and the earth billions of years ago; but all life, including humans, evolved over millions of years from earlier life forms due to environmental pressures to adapt and without any guidance from God or an intelligent force)
- Natural evolution (a purely evolutionary explanation of human origins and a universe that began billions of years ago without any help from a creator God)

Using these six narratives rather than a strictly binary choice changed the picture that emerged. There is no question that the vast majority of scientists accept the theory of evolution. My survey of academic scientists in eight nations found that

92 percent believe that humans evolved over time.[1] Yet when I asked scientists who work outside elite universities (those who work as engineers or in research and development, for example) to choose between the six narratives of human origins, natural evolution—evolution with no involvement from God or a higher power—was the *least* popular.[2] In fact, 70 percent of these scientists said that the narrative that all life, including humans, evolved over millions of years *without* the involvement of God or an intelligent force was probably or definitely *false*. In other words, many scientists accept evolution while also maintaining that a creator God played some role in creation.

When I presented the six different narratives to evangelical Christians across the US and asked them to what extent they thought each was true or false, a little less than 40 percent said young-earth creationism—the idea that God created everything within the past ten thousand years—is definitely true.[3] When I looked at US evangelical *scientists* outside of universities, a little less than 35 percent said they thought the narrative that God created the universe, the earth, and all of life within the past ten thousand years was definitely true.

Yet that was only part of the story. While young-earth creationism was the most popular narrative among evangelicals, I found that almost 40 percent of evangelical Christians were unwilling to commit as a "true believer" to any single perspective on the origin and development of life.[4] A number of evangelicals displayed dynamic rather than static beliefs. Yvonne, for example, who emphasized in our discussion her unwavering conviction that "God created *everything*," later admitted that she still feels some uncertainty about how everything came to be and that she is not quite sure whether she believes evolution was the way God created or if it was some other way. "Some things are always a mystery, and none of us will ever know everything," she said, "but it is by faith that you believe that."[5]

One of the most interesting things I found was that many religious believers, especially evangelical Christians, simultaneously hold contradictory views on human origins. For example, a number of individuals who said young-earth creationism is "definitely true" also said that it is "definitely true" that "God created the universe and the earth billions of years ago; God started and has guided human evolution over millions of years." In fact, 30 percent of evangelicals in my research said they viewed multiple origin narratives, narratives that contradict one another, as being "definitely true."[6]

In other words, many Christians are unsure what to believe when it comes to explanations for the origin of the universe and the development of life on earth, oftentimes grappling with how to balance their faith with the evidence for the theory of evolution. Some Christians treat the creation account in Genesis as an important story that is "true" in a moral rather than literal sense, and thus they can also accept the scientific explanation of evolution as true in a factual way.[7] Others reconcile evolution with their faith by concluding that God utilized evolution to develop life on earth. Blythe, for example, a professor who studies the brain and the nervous system, said she accepts the biblical story of creation by interpreting the "days" of creation as "creative periods." She understands, however, that it is not easy for other members of her church to let go of their more "dogmatic" views. "I think a lot of people have the fear that, you know, [finding out about evolution] is going to degrade the basis of what they believe in, and that's frightening for a lot of people because they've been taught these things their whole life and put their stock in them," she said. "It's hard to let go of that."[8]

For some evangelical Christians, the most important consideration when contemplating narratives to explain the origin of the universe and the development of life on earth is whether the narrative accounts for what they view as important theological beliefs—namely, a creator role for God and a relationship between God and humans. For example, evangelical Christians are much more likely than Catholics or Jews to believe that God is "directly involved in the affairs of the world." They also care very deeply about protecting the idea that humans are created in the image of God and thus hold a special place in creation. A number of evangelical Christians are open to other explanations for the development of life besides strict creationism if these explanations do not rule out human uniqueness.

My research has found that Christians who understand the science of evolutionary theory can be held back from fully accepting the theory because they fear its theological implications—specifically, what it means for God's role in the world and the specialness of human beings. I have interviewed many Christians who voiced concerns about what evolution means for the nature of God as revealed in the Bible, and my research shows that many Christians have trouble accepting evolution if they believe it eliminates a creator role for God. The "idea of a Creator—'Was a Creator behind evolution?' or 'Is there a Creator or not?'—is more important," said an evangelical Christian who is in medical school. "Could a Creator have used evolution as a means to create man or something? Sure. Why not? But I think 'Is there a Creator?' is a much more important question."[9]

Who Is God in Evolutionary Theory?

"To me, the theory of evolution takes God out of it," said a woman whose evangelical church in Houston participated in one of my studies.[10] And a Christian woman from Chicago told me, "I don't think you can explain creation using any part of the theory of evolution because evolution is not encompassing the fact that there was a supernatural being that just created everything. . . . It's like a total opposite."[11]

I have spent a lot of time exploring the website BioLogos, founded by Francis Collins, who currently directs the National Institutes of Health. BioLogos is one of the most prominent programs working to help Christians "see the harmony between science and biblical faith," and it presents "an evolutionary understanding of God's creation." In his book *The Language of God*, Collins writes,

> If humans evolved strictly by mutation and natural selection, who needs God to explain us? To this, I reply: I do. The comparison of chimp and human sequences, interesting as it is, does not tell us what it means to be human. In my views, DNA sequence alone, even if accompanied by a vast trove of data on biological function, will never explain certain special human attributes, such as the knowledge of the Moral Law and the universal search for God. Freeing God from the burden of special acts of creation does not remove Him as the source of the things that make humanity special, and of the universe itself. It merely shows us something of how He operates.[12]

In an essay for BioLogos, Ryan Bebej, a Christian professor of biology at Calvin University, reflects on his transition from being a young-earth creationist to becoming an evolution expert. "Previously, I had this notion that new discoveries in science were a threat to God—as if God resides in the mysteries of the universe, and any time we figure out something new, we make God a little bit smaller," he writes. "Following this logic, eventually scientific progress would result in a God so small that we could discard him completely." Yet as Bebej considered and came to understand the evidence for evolution, he became "especially interested in trying to figure out whether or not this science could fit with [his] faith." He began to see "that there were a number of ways that Christians could deal with the scientific evidence and that working as a scientist did not necessitate a loss of faith." He explains, "I started to get this sense that I truly saw God in the details, in the complex inner-workings of natural processes. My view of God seemed to be getting bigger and bigger the more I understood about how the material world works."[13]

Like Bebej, many Christians I've spoken with see the theory of evolution as compatible with their belief in God and have found that the more they learn about the beauty and order of the natural world through science, the better they feel they understand God's character. Jaime, the Christian evolutionary biologist we met earlier, explained how evolution draws her closer to God and gives her a better sense of the special place of humans in the creation. She sees evolution as full of beautiful patterns and as a facet of how God created and sustains the world. Her evolutionary research serves to *strengthen* her faith. She said, "I'm working very hard to understand the social implications of the ideas that we have where we separate the natural from the supernatural . . . trying to understand how God is at work within those natural processes, so that we don't tip into kind of a deism perspective, where God isn't actively engaged. Those are the types of questions that . . . deepen my faith and of course deepen my understanding of how God does work in the world."[14] Kurt, an evangelical Christian who is a research physician, also maintains, like Jaime, that evolution strengthens his faith. For him, evolution shows that all of us as God's children are linked to each other. It means "fundamentally that we're related to each other . . . which to me is a beautiful description," he said.[15] Accepting the science of evolution does not preclude him from continuing to find meaning in the story of creation. He told me, "Evolution and evolution of the world, or creation of the world and the evolution of life and human beings, has informed my understanding of biblical creation stories. I think I can interpret the Bible, and I think that the Bible will continue to have valuable messages and meanings that concern humans for at least hundreds of years, if not thousands of years to come." He goes on to say, "Will those understandings change? Yes. But they've changed before, and they'll continue to change. . . . I fully recognize that ten years or a hundred years from now we may have a very different date on the age of the earth, on the age of the universe, and I think that both the scientists and the religious people are going to have to adjust to those things."[16]

Kurt remembers his father explaining to him the significance of the work of Louis Leakey, a pioneer in the study of early human evolution, and how evolution strengthened the scientist's faith. "Leakey was being interviewed. . . . He was talking about how he never considered any of his discoveries to be particularly in conflict with any biblical tradition or religious views, [but that we have] a God-given ability . . . to discover the world around us and interpret it," Kurt recalled. "And it augmented [Leakey's] belief in religion rather than contradicting it."[17] As another scientist I interviewed told me, "The fact that the creation could be set up in such a way that hominids could evolve through the process of natural selection does not seem at all incompatible with either God's sovereignty over the creation or the critical role of the sort of unique relationship of human beings with the creator."[18]

In my research and discussions with Christians, I have heard several other ways in which people reconcile evolution with their faith. Some Christians accept evolution through the concept of "evolution with a divine first cause,"[19] meaning they believe evolution would not have been possible without God, who was the starting point, creating initial life on earth before the natural processes of evolution took over. One Christian woman explained her belief this way: "There is nobody who knows how any of this got here. There was nothing and there was something. What happened between nothing and something? You have to start with something to evolve into something else. So where did the something come from? It didn't evolve out of nothing. It started. Evolution requires a starting point. You can't change something that isn't there."[20]

Other Christians I spoke with think God can continue to be involved in the process of evolution. Some Christians believe God not only initiated the process but also constantly and deliberately guides it. One Christian I spoke with told me he believes evolution leaves room for God's ongoing involvement in the world:

> Evolution to me is a really broad term; you could look at all animal and plant life and things change over time and they adapt. . . . And I'm not struggling too much with that. If it had to be my guess, that's what God planned, and that we didn't just evolve one day and that was it. That there's been an evolutionary process and we're part of it. And instead of fighting it, I think it's really fascinating how it's come about. And did one day God really suddenly inject knowledge in a way that allowed us to evolve in a different way? Maybe. I'm just not too worried about [answering] that. I think God's here.[21]

Where Are Humans in Evolutionary Theory?

Many Christians feel that accepting evolution means abandoning the idea of *imago Dei*—that humans are created in God's image. As writer Richard Ostling puts it, "The emerging science could be seen to challenge not only what Genesis records about the creation of humanity but the species' unique status as bearing the 'image of God.'"[22]

Based on my research, it seems Christians have different reasons for placing great importance on the belief that humans are created in the image of God. Some talked about the importance of this doctrine for finding meaning and purpose in living a virtuous life. "If I am created by God, in God's image, in His likeness, and I'm given a purpose, I have a reason for living. . . . I help other people not to make myself look better or to feel better," a Christian man told me. "[I help others] because [I want to] glorify the one who created me, in His image."[23] For this man, being made in the image of God gave him a reason to strive toward a virtuous life. I heard something similar from many other Christians, including a geneticist who said, "You're bringing honor to God by pursuing excellence and representing and reflecting Him well. And I think that's what matters more, so I think we all have that shared calling of being made in the image of God. That's our calling. It's to reflect Him. It's to represent Him."[24]

Some Christians make a distinction between microevolution and macroevolution, accepting the former and dismissing the latter. These Christians usually feel very comfortable with microevolution, which refers to changes within a species over time, and they acknowledge that evidence for it has been produced in the lab. Yet they are often uncomfortable with the idea of macroevolution, which refers to changes across species and finds support in the fossil record. For these Christians, the problem with macroevolution is the notion that humans evolved from "lesser" species, which challenges the idea that humans were made directly by God in God's image. "I'm not denying that . . . maybe there is some form of evolution that happened, but I can't get on board with the idea that humans weren't originally humans. I believe that humans were always humans," one Christian woman told me.[25]

"There's the side of it that looks at what makes humans special. Is it nothing, as some of the brashest scientists would say?" one professor of physical chemistry said. "If I accept evolution, does that undermine everything I think about humans and the Christian story?"[26] For those who worry that without the biblical first human, the entire Christian story collapses, Greg Cootsona, who teaches religion at California State University at Chico, helpfully reminds them in his book *Mere Science and Christian Faith* that "the center of our faith is Christ, not

Adam."[27] Ultimately, the image of God is most clearly realized in the person of Jesus Christ, and thus evolutionary accounts of human origins do not have to be a threat to our understanding of what it means to be endowed with the image of God.

The Christian woman I mentioned earlier who attends the Chicago church told me she chose her "religious belief over the science of evolution" because "nobody could ever explain that to me—how, as intricate as our bodies are, as intricate as the world is, how it can just be made from a big bang. It just . . . never made sense."[28] For some Christians, the idea of creation without a higher purpose feels wrong, and they dismiss the theory of evolution on that basis. One Christian wondered, "Was [human life] just a random product of random particles bouncing together and growing from a single cell to complex cells? . . . It could be, but my experience in life doesn't seem to allude to that kind of idea."[29] An evangelical Christian pastor told me that in her view "the evolution premise as a whole, the idea that random mutations, and like an error here and an error here, led to human beings who are so bent on anything but randomness, who are all about purpose and meaning and questions of 'why?' I just don't see how totally random processes could have gotten us here, if that makes sense."[30]

Because my survey offered Christians six narratives to describe their views about evolution rather than asking them to choose only one, they could share their thoughts in a deep and detailed way. I have uncovered the following key takeaways as a result of this.

For one, many Christians are able to accept the idea that life on earth evolved over time if they are given the opportunity to also express the idea that God plays some role in the process of evolution.

My research also showed me that science does not seem safe for everyone. I found that members of Christian communities that historically (and sometimes even today) have been seen as inferior because of the color of their skin had concerns about evolution and racism. David Unander, a professor of biology whose work examines race, explains, "By the late 1800s, evolution was the metaphor for 'eugenics,' a program to eliminate inferiors within European nations, while promoting superior types, but also to eventually eliminate inferior peoples worldwide."[31] In this way, ideas about evolution were linked to ideas about racial superiority. In black and Latino/a communities, then, harboring suspicion toward scientists (and toward medicine) can be part of a "community of memory,"[32] where even if an individual has not herself experienced marginalization or discrimination at the hands of science, her community supports a narrative that suggests such abuses might happen.

It is important to emphasize here that while evolution has been invoked to support prejudice, it is not a cause; there is nothing about the descriptive process of evolution per se that leads to racism or eugenics. This link is one that was twisted and perverted by others for their own aims. At the same time, this perversion continues to have an impact on perceptions of science among members of color in Christian communities who fear that it may be used as a tool to diminish their humanity.

One pastor at a black church described how difficult it can be for members of his church to accept evolution, given how it has been wielded against them by those who have perverted the ideas behind the theory: "[Scientists] know we didn't come from a monkey. And these people [people in my church—a black church] have been told that that's precisely where they've come from. Right? And they know that the stuff that folks have been saying about them ever since they've been in this country is not true. They know that. And they will scoff at it."[33]

When I spoke with other pastors in low-income, underserved communities composed of people of color, they also told me their congregants simply don't spend much time thinking about how to reconcile their Christian beliefs with the theory of evolution. They have more pressing human needs. One pastor of a predominantly black church in an impoverished metropolitan area told me with a laugh,

> I think for most people within my congregation they are not dealing with [evolution] but the routine of living. If you're a senior and you've got money, you're dealing with health. If you're young and got health, then you're dealing with wealth issues. . . . Then you've got individuals who are dealing with social dysfunction, criminal behavior and activities, and things of that nature. . . . And so they're dealing with probation officers and inability to get a job because they have a record. . . . And so to sit around and have a conversation about "What do you think about evolution?" is to say, "What in the hell is wrong with you?"[34]

Finally, for those Christians who are struggling to reconcile evolution with their religious beliefs, it can be helpful to hear from other Christians who have found ways to accept evolution while maintaining belief in a creator God, and church should be a place where they can share their approaches to evolution. It can also be helpful for Christians to consider the crucial and immutable beliefs underlying the biblical creation story and to ask themselves which, if any, are at stake or must be abandoned if they accept the evidence for evolution.

Questions about the role God plays in evolution are difficult questions. We can find some guidance by looking at how committed Christians who are also scientists tackle these issues. Some, like Christian physicist Loren Haarsma, see orderliness in evolution and believe it displays the fingerprints of God. "God created biological information through evolutionary mechanisms in ways analogous to how God creates the information needed to describe each new snowflake, each new tree, each new ecosystem, and every new human being," he explains.[35]

Christians can also recognize that evolutionary theory supports many ideas that are a valued part of the Christian faith—

ideas related to human connectedness and human uniqueness in our capacity for a particular kind of human love, cooperation, altruism, and thought. Evolution shows us that we humans are special. Evolutionary scientists and Christians can join together in recognizing the importance of curiosity and creativity for humanness. The physicist Mario Livio writes, "The ability for creative thinking, which is largely powered by curiosity, coupled with the aptness to share accumulated knowledge and to pool intelligence with others, eventually led to a few spectacular developments in the history of humankind."[36] It is to virtues like curiosity and creativity that we now turn.

Further Discussion

1. What significance does being made in the image of God (the *imago Dei*) hold for your life?
2. How do you think about the creation account in Genesis 1–2? Did the Christians introduced in this chapter offer you new ways to think about the relationship between the biblical creation account and evolution?
3. How do you feel about the idea of "theistic evolution"—evolution that is initiated or guided by God?
4. To what extent do you think it's important to educate Christians on evolution? What would be the best way to do so?

PART 2

PROCESS

4

Curiosity

YOU REMEMBER some conversations for the rest of your life. When I met Jill, she was already at the top of her field, a biologist leading a successful laboratory at an elite research university.[1] As I walked toward her office, I noticed her door had a sign of the Darwin fish eating the Christian fish (the ichthus symbol). I was conducting my first study on scientists' attitudes toward faith, and the sign made me nervous. I knocked tentatively. Maybe it would be OK if Jill had forgotten the appointment for our interview, I thought. But she came to the door right away.

Jill did nothing to put me at ease. She did not greet me with a handshake or a smile. Instead, she curtly asked me to come in and directed me to sit on a metal chair across the desk from her. She told me she had nothing to say about science and faith. She was participating in my study only because, as a researcher herself, she wanted to support research. I cannot remember now if the air conditioning in her office was on full blast or if I just felt cold.

Even in that first year of my research, I noticed that scientists were responding to my study in vastly different ways. Sometimes their busy careers meant they had no time to talk about existential things. Others seemed as if they had been waiting all their lives to have a conversation about the big questions and meaning of life. Others were deeply uncomfortable or hostile. Sitting in Jill's office, I assumed I needed to steel myself for one of those harder conversations.

I told Jill a little about my study; I explained that I was a sociologist who wanted to move beyond anecdotes and stereotypes to study systematically for the first time what scientists think about faith and what people from different religious traditions think about science. Then I asked Jill if she practiced a religion or considered herself a person of faith. "No. I am simply an atheist," she responded tersely. I then asked whether she had been raised in a faith tradition. It was the type of question that could have been answered yes or no.

I was taken aback when Jill looked away from me and her eyes began to fill with tears. In the years since then, I have interviewed more than a thousand scientists about their views on faith; Jill is one of the only ones who cried. As her tears welled up, my own feelings turned from apprehension to compassion. I also wanted to know more about why the question about her faith background elicited such emotion.

Jill told me that she came from a Christian family and, as a child, had spent a lot of time at church. Raised in a rural community, Jill also spent a lot of time outdoors, and she began to see the beauty in nature and to develop a real love of the natural world. She spent a lot of time on her schoolwork too; she particularly loved her biology and chemistry classes. She was a "total geek," she said, and her grades were "fantabulous." She thought she might become a teacher or a doctor.

But as she became more curious about the natural world, Jill also became concerned about aspects of her faith. For instance, while scientists had determined that the earth is billions of years old, her church was part of the community of Christians who read the Bible as teaching that the earth was created by God in its present form just thousands of years ago. She brought questions about the origin and development of life on earth and the role of God in creation to her parents and her pastors. Jill was also curious about whether Christians could be scientists.

At that point, Jill did not know she would go into science and she was not yet considering whether she would remain part of a church. Church and school were both central to her life. She was simply an inquisitive kid, following and feeding her natural curiosity. But "when I asked hard questions, I was told by my pastor just to make a decision to believe . . . to forget about science," she said. It was an answer that did not satisfy Jill. She tried several times to talk with her youth group leaders about the questions science brought to mind, but her experiences with them were similar; she was consistently told not to explore so much. "I feel like religion was a mechanism by which judgment was passed on people who were different," she recounted. "And for me, in my personal history in my childhood, it was judgment. It didn't work out so well for me." By the time Jill was in her teens, she had left her church.

Sometimes, even now, she said, she yearns for a sense of what it would mean to have faith. "What is it that keeps people believing? I feel like when religion works you get a sense of community," she said. "You get a way to teach morality and ethics in the sense of how you teach someone the difference between right and wrong. But when it doesn't work it just turns into judgment."

Nurturing Curiosity

"As a character trait," the philosopher Elias Baumgarten writes, "curiosity is a disposition to want to know or learn more about a wide variety of things. The more one has this character trait, the more often or the more intensely one will on particular occasions experience a desire or urge to investigate and learn more about something."[2]

In our current culture, being *curious* is undervalued. It brings to mind a child wondering what is around the corner before she takes a look. Our culture prefers seemingly stronger roles like being an *expert* or being a *leader*. We often want to be next to people who seem like they already know the whole truth. Curiosity is a fundamental value of my own discipline; at its core, sociology is about listening carefully and being curious about other people and their stories. I highly value the ability to ask questions that help us better understand both others and ourselves and that help us lead better lives.[3] I see curiosity—when used wisely—as a show of strength, a yearning to push the boundaries of knowledge.

Scientists like Jill are often known for their curiosity. Albert Einstein said, "I have no special talents. I am only passionately curious."[4] The physicist Mario Livio, in his well-known book *Why? What Makes Us Curious*, argues that the best scientists are passionately curious, often in several different domains. Fabiola Gianotti, the first woman to serve as director-general of CERN, the famous European Organization for Nuclear Research, told Livio that first she was passionately curious about music and only later did she switch from studying the humanities to studying physics: "I was always a curious child. . . . I always had many questions. At one point I decided that physics will actually allow me to try to *answer* some of those questions."[5] And the most successful scientists report that their curiosity was nurtured from a very young age, often by their families and larger communities. For example, the string theorist Sylvester James Gates Jr., the first African American to have an endowed chair in physics at a major research university, speaks publicly about the relationship between religion and science. Gates says that he got used to being curious, to asking hard questions at an early age: "I remember once I asked [my dad], 'Dad, do you remember me as a kid asking all kinds of questions?' and he said, 'yes.' I said, 'you always had answers for everything.' And he said, 'yes.' I said, 'How did you do that?' and he said, 'What you don't remember son, is if I didn't have an answer immediately I would tell you hold off, and I would go and get some resource and in the next day or so I'd come back and answer your question.'" Even though no one in Gates's family was a scientist, they created an environment that nurtured his curiosity.[6]

For some in the Christian community, curiosity can sometimes seem risky or scary. When Jill brought her questions about faith to her parents and pastors, her curiosity elicited fear. As a parent and member of a church community, I identify to an extent with Jill's parents and pastors. I think about the kinds of questions about science and faith my own daughter might have some day and how they might impact her relationship with our faith. But as someone who had her own questions about the relationship of science and faith as a child, I can identify with Jill's curiosity as well. As someone who also left a church when her questions and quest for knowledge were dismissed or discouraged, Jill helped me realize how important it is to nurture curiosity as a virtue in our faith communities.

In fact, Christianity calls us to be curious. One of my favorite verses in the Bible is Philippians 4:8: "Finally, brothers and sisters, whatever is true, whatever is noble, whatever is right, whatever is pure, whatever is lovely [or beautiful], whatever is admirable—if anything is excellent or praiseworthy—think about such things." As Greg Cootsona writes, "Whatever human knowledge discovers in nature, we are bound to listen, to learn, and to engage with it. Why? Because God has spoken and continues to speak through Scripture and through the natural world—through both words and works—albeit in different modes."[7]

Getting Curious

In the churches I visited during my studies, I heard many Christians express fear of scientists. They believe all scientists are atheists and hostile to religion. They hear a lot from the New Atheists, a small but outspoken group led by scientists who are anti-religion and argue that science and religion are inherently in conflict. For a number of Christians, the New Atheists actually stifle curiosity about science and its relationship to faith and create rigid boundaries between the scientific and faith communities. Moreover, many Christians also told me their pastors or church leaders never talk about science. This, too, can suppress curiosity.

It is time we honor curiosity about science in church. Interpreted from a Christian perspective, science can be seen as a tool to pursue knowledge and truth about creation and to better understand the words and works of God and how we can live better lives.

My husband, Karl, and I are both professors who have devoted our careers to science. Karl is a particle physicist, and between us, we have nearly twenty years of higher-education and postdoctoral training in the natural and social sciences. About ten years ago, when Karl and I learned that we were going to have a baby, we did what came naturally to us as scientists. We applied our scientific and academic training and skills. We read and studied *a lot* of books about babies and childcare. In this way, we thought we could learn the whole truth about child rearing before our child arrived.

Then our daughter was born. For about three weeks after Anika arrived, we always had at least one family member with us who could provide support. Then they all left. We were alone and afraid. That first night, we experienced our first test. Anika would not stop crying. We did everything the books suggested: we checked for gas and burped her, checked for fever, and changed her diaper. This all led to severe distress on her part—to the point where projectile matter ended up both on us and on the wall next to her changing table, and we had to use some cloth diapers to wipe down ourselves and the wall with disinfectant. She kept crying. Both my husband (the very smart particle physicist) and I (the sociologist, who is supposed to have some special intellectual insight into the human condition) had sweat from the stress pouring off our faces. We were two adults who had not slept in twenty-four hours, and we were using the remaining clean cloth diapers to wipe our dripping brows.

We had done everything we had read that we should do, and nothing had worked. We became convinced that we must have missed a crucial piece of information in one of the baby-care manuals, that our level of study had not been enough. I turned to my husband and said, "Go get the baby book." We were going to read our way out of it!

Today, with some years of parenting under my belt, I chuckle when I think about that night and our belief that all we needed was the right passage in a book. Our studying helped feed what Mario Livio calls "epistemic curiosity," a desire to learn new knowledge. What we needed that evening, however, was a better way to address what he calls "perceptual curiosity." Perceptual curiosity is "the curiosity we feel when something surprises us or when something doesn't quite agree with what we know or think we know." He writes, "That is felt as an unpleasant state, as an adversity state. It's a bit like an itch that we need to scratch. That's why we try to find out the information in order to relieve that type of curiosity."[8] That night we did not need to be curious about the words in a book; we needed to be more curious about the peculiarities of our particular child.

I now believe that on that night with Anika, I should have turned to another mother or father, to a member of my community, to someone who had experience and expertise raising a child, to ask them questions and listen to their perspective.

This would have been the best way to get the information we needed to solve our problems and alleviate our fears.

My research shows that many Christians are curious about the relationship between science and religion and how they can integrate science with their faith. This curiosity can be painful and stressful. In one study, Livio writes, researchers showed that "perceptual curiosity appeared to produce a negative feeling of need and deprivation, something akin to thirst."[9] Satisfying this curiosity, the research showed, can feel like a reward. Christian communities can become safe places for the curious, especially those who are curious about science and faith. The most valuable resource in the Christian community is the believers who have personal experience and accomplishment, the fellow Christians who have successfully integrated science and faith before the youth in their churches. From these Christians, we can learn new ways of looking at the relationship between religion and science and why curiosity for science should be fostered and supported within the church. Churches need to become places that offer the reward of nurturing and satisfying curiosity, where Christians can reduce the conflict and stress they feel when thinking about the relationship between science and faith. Curiosity is a necessary part of the process of scientific discovery *and* of understanding the interface between science and faith. But for many, curiosity leads to doubts about faith.

Further Discussion

1. What role do you think God played in creating science? What scientific idea do you wish you knew more about?
2. How are you exploring the relationship between faith and science? Have you discovered any tensions that you are working through?

3. How could your congregation better nurture curious exploration of science?
4. How could your congregation better nurture curious exploration of faith?
5. What is your faith community doing to nurture the curiosity of children?

5

Doubt

> Now Thomas . . . , one of the Twelve, was not with the disciples when Jesus came. So the other disciples told him, "We have seen the Lord!" But he said to them, "Unless I see the nail marks in his hands and put my finger where the nails were, and put my hand into his side, I will not believe."
>
> John 20:24–25

CONVENTIONAL THINKING is that science relies on reason and evidence, while religion relies on faith. Science means *doubting* first, until we can explain by seeing, while faith is the substance of things hoped for, the evidence of things *not seen*, according to the writer of Hebrews (Heb. 11:1).

In the scientific community, doubt is not only useful but also essential. Curiosity allows scientists to question the world around them, even the parts of it we often take for granted, and to discover new insights. But curiosity about a new thing often leads scientists to *doubt* a discovery of the past. Robert K.

Merton, a sociologist of science who taught at Columbia University, argued that one of the key group norms of science is what he called "organized skepticism," which is the idea that science is organized in part around scientists having detached scrutiny of their work and suspending their own judgment to get to the scientific truth. In other words, Merton argues, science is based on experiencing doubt.[1]

Religious systems, however, are often seen as ways of lessening doubt. In Christianity, "doubting Thomas," of the biblical story quoted in part above, is generally used in sermons as an exemplar of what *not* to be.[2] Christians are often encouraged to protect their faith from sources of doubt: "Going back to the days of Darwin there has always been a conflict [between science and faith]," one woman told me during a study I did on how religious people understand science. She continued, "I don't know if it's a . . . deliberate attempt to cast doubt or plant the seed of doubt. Being a spiritual person, I know that there's also an evil spirit that's there. It can kind of work to cast doubt in a person's mind. And so Darwinism has been one of the tools, one of the things that's aided doubt."[3] In this way, science has often been seen as a threat to faith.

But what if we Christians began to look at doubt differently—as useful, under certain conditions, rather than as something to be feared or suppressed or avoided? In their book, *In Praise of Doubt*, the late sociologist Peter Berger and the philosopher Anton Zijderveld write, "If people converse with each other over time, they begin to influence each other's thinking. As such 'contamination' occurs, people find it more and more difficult to characterize the beliefs and values of the others as perverse. . . . Slowly but surely, the thought obtrudes that, maybe, these people have a point."[4] Contamination, it seems, is precisely what some Christians I have interviewed are afraid of. But what if we see doubt as possibly leading to more robust faith? Doubt is an essential part of Anselm of Canterbury's (ca. 1033–1109) dictum *fides quaurens intellectum*, faith seeking understanding.[5] This is the theological method stressed earlier by Augustine (ca. 354–430) in which we begin in faith, then move to further understanding through seeking, questioning, and *doubting*.

Like these theologians, I believe doubt can be a strength and a virtue in Christian communities, just as it is in the scientific community, and that recognizing doubt as a virtue can help us become more open to science and to reconciling science with our faith. I also believe church communities can be productive places—perhaps the *most* productive places—to wrestle with doubts raised by science, allowing us to explore those doubts in ways that lead to greater acceptance of science and a stronger, more resilient faith.

My own journey toward harmonizing religion and science began with a crisis of doubt. I was ten years old when I noticed that I could no longer make a fist. Over time, my feet started to swell and walking became painful if I stood for more than an hour. Yet my face looked like that of a healthy child. It took nearly a year of medical tests and visits to specialists before I was given the diagnosis of "undiagnosed mixed connective tissue disease." My disease looked something like juvenile rheumatoid arthritis and something like scleroderma, a disease that had recently become well known after it had taken the life of a movie star's sister.

My doctors told my family that before I turned twenty I would probably lose the ability to walk, to carry a stack of books, and to have children. Then my spine began to contort. I was eleven years old when I was diagnosed with scoliosis, a curvature of the spine. When I was thirteen, they made me a back brace that I wore twenty-two hours a day in an effort to keep my spine from growing in a crooked direction. I remember the casting process to stabilize my spine: I put on a thin body stocking and the technician applied plaster to my entire body; then, to make the mold, he smoothed the plaster with strong strokes around my midsection. After about an hour of smoothing, the casting technician cut off the outer cast, and I was left standing in the thin body stocking.

I entered high school with that brace under my clothes. If I stood perfectly straight with a stiff upper body, no one could see it. But if I dropped something on the floor and bent to pick it up, they would see the brace jut out at the top of my shirt. I went to great lengths not to let anything drop to the ground, and I developed entirely new skill sets. In band, for example, a small breeze would blow through the room when the teacher opened the window, and sometimes this would cause our sheet music to fall off its stand. I played mallet percussion (like the xylophone) and became adept at catching my sheet music between my mallets before it could fall. The surgery to treat my scoliosis took place nearly thirty years ago now, and my only physical reminder is a thin, six-inch scar on my back.

Back then, as part of a conservative Baptist family, I began to have questions about both faith and science as my illness progressed. I questioned whether I could trust doctors and scientists (some members of my family did not, while other members revered them). I questioned whether I could trust a God who would let the health of a preteen crumble. I wondered what science could tell me about whether I could lead a normal life in the midst of my disease, have children, or even live at all. I definitely did not feel like church was a safe place to ask these sorts of questions or to explore my doubt, and this feeling eventually led me to leave my church. Through my research, I have discovered that my childhood experience was not unique. Fear of doubt is present in many church contexts.

Despite what medical science predicted about me, I ran track in high school. Despite what sociologists predict about kids who leave church when doubts about faith are not dealt with, I did make my way back. Today, I can walk, carry books, and if you visit me on a Sunday morning, you will likely find my daughter running around in our church with a gang of her friends.

I no longer doubt the power of medicine. I have had six surgeries related to my disease, including two hip replacements. Yet doctors often look at my medical chart and prognosis and tell me, "You are a walking miracle." There are people in my church who think that—at least as far as my physical body goes—I might just be one. I've met Christian doctors who believe God could have helped heal me completely, either through the medical tools they see as gifts from God or through the doctors they believe are called by God to serve. Some believe I have experienced divine healing. Some wonder why there are days I still limp. Other doctors doubt the power of faith. They talk to me about how prognoses change, or they predict that the disease will still take a turn for the worse.

Moving Past Conflict

A few years back, as part of research I was conducting, I sat in on a group meeting in a rural church in the farm country of upstate New York. One of the women asked me what I did for work, and I told her I was a doctoral student at Cornell University. "Yuck," she replied. "I wouldn't want my children to attend Cornell." I was shocked. Most people think of Cornell as a top school. When I asked her to explain her reaction, she told me she wouldn't want her children to go to Cornell because they might be exposed to scientists who would raise doubts in their fragile young minds that would take them away from their faith.

Pastors often avoid topics related to science or to the relationship between Christianity and science. They worry that exposure to science—specifically certain scientific findings and ideas that might seem to contradict religious ideas—will cause Christians to begin to doubt aspects of their faith and eventually lead them away from their faith. But I have found that when Christian parents and pastors try to "protect" kids from doubt by keeping them from exploring or understanding scientific ideas, they may actually be driving them away from the church. These youth miss the opportunity to experience *prudent doubt*, to openly wrestle with their faith in a way that will lead both to more openness toward science and to a stronger faith.

I have also found that Christians who do not talk about science at church are usually left to believe what the loudest voices tell them: that all Christians are anti-science and all scientists are anti-Christian. The media often tells us that most Christians, especially evangelical Christians, reject science. More specifically, we hear that Christians ignore scientific evidence, are hostile to evolution, are skeptical of climate change, and oppose biomedical technologies. Christianity is often presented as a religion that does not permit doubt, resulting in followers that trust in silly things that are sometimes anti-science.

Despite these perceptions, when I interviewed Christians about science and the relationship between science and their religious beliefs, I discovered a much different reality. I met Christians who were very open about experiencing doubt when thinking about the relationship between science and their faith. I remember one evangelical Christian math teacher in particular. She argued that we should not be afraid of doubt. In her view, doubt is a natural human response and, wrestled with rightly, can be a human virtue. What's more, she believed that doubt should be honestly expressed in the safety of Christian communities. "To be honest, I've doubted, OK? I've woken up and doubted, 'Is there a God? Is there really a God? Is what I believe really true? This sounds crazy. A man died and rose again? Who believes that?'" she said. "Everyone, I think, has had doubts before, but I think that the thing is, I doubt my doubts. And I believe that I didn't just conjure up this faith. I believe God gave me faith."[6]

Boundary Pioneers

In my research, I have met evangelical Christians who ignore scientific evidence and are hostile to science, but I have also met many others who have found ways to work through the doubts science raises about their religious beliefs, ultimately accepting science and remaining staunch in their faith. Some see science as a tool or a calling that helps them better understand God's work. Many find that it provides support for their faith.

I think we need to show how science can bolster faith (which is not the same thing as certainty). The boundary pioneers—scientists who are committed Christians and who break down the boundary between science and religion, those who live in both worlds—are our models. They show us that scientific evidence has actually opened up their faith to mystery and awe. They show us that faith doesn't have to equal certainty; faith can *include* or coexist with doubt, with critical questions, and with shifts in perspective as more information comes to light.

For example, my studies show that nearly 50 percent of evangelicals believe that science and religion can work together and support each other, and 67 percent of evangelical scientists believe science and religion can be collaborative. "Science is fantastic and I thank God for this," one evangelical Christian said. "It isn't as if He didn't want us to find out about His incredible creation."[7]

My research also shows that scientists in the US are far more religious than the stereotypes often presented in the media would have us think. Among what I call "rank and file scientists" (those who work outside of top research universities), 65 percent identify as Christian and almost 21 percent as evangelical.[8] Among scientists working at universities and colleges, nearly a quarter identify as Christian. Of this group of Christian university scientists, more than 80 percent attend church, nearly 84 percent pray, and 58 percent affirm the authority or inspiration of the Bible.[9]

Scientists who identify as Christian often believe their faith bolsters their scientific work, and some see it as adding meaning to their discoveries. Some also believe science can strengthen faith. "I don't see science as an occupation," an evangelical biologist told me. "I see it as a cathedral where I come to worship God."[10] Explaining how she sees God's work in her research and how this strengthens her Christian faith, a professor of genetics told me, "It is the word of God and his laws that are reflected in the very sequence, the patterns, the sequences of the genome that give expression to biology as we study it."[11]

I met Blythe (the professor I introduced earlier who studies the brain and nervous system) one Sunday morning at a women's Bible study group. She believes that her faith influences everything she does and how she perceives the world. Even though some people at her church have had trouble believing that she can be both a Christian and a scientist, she feels that her scientific work actually affirms her belief in God. She told me,

> You look at DNA or at neurologic systems, and you look at the amount of order that is actually in those systems, it's just remarkable. . . . Things generally become less ordered; they degrade and they become more random . . . so to think that things could become more ordered . . . goes against one of the basic premises of science, and so you have to think, "How did this just happen? How did all this order occur randomly?" Because it's not how we think of things working. And so, somebody who doesn't have a faith background doesn't really understand that perhaps there's a Creator, someone who created all the order.[12]

Scientists who are Christians can help their fellow Christians enter the realm of science and see how it can help us further express, use, and live out our faith. Christian scientists can also help young Christians—especially those who might be considering entry into scientific or technological occupations—figure out how to approach commonly perceived conflicts between science and religion and see how scientific work can be a kind of mission or calling.

As I mentioned earlier, for the past four years, I have led a program on faith and science in the church I attend in Houston, Texas. There are about four hundred people in the congregation, which is considered small- to medium-sized in Texas. (In upstate New York, where I was raised, a four-hundred-person church would have been considered a megachurch!) I have also shared some of my research on Christianity and science in my church and in other churches throughout the US. I have found that congregations thirst for dialogue on science and religion, to hear what their fellow Christians believe and how they reconcile their faith with science. Congregants are looking for guidance when it comes to integrating science with their faith.

In surveying and interviewing hundreds of Christians, I have also found that they are often looking for a safe place to express doubts, including those raised by science. I think about a geneticist who told me he often felt lonely as a committed Christian who was in graduate school in the sciences at an elite university.[13] He longed for a local church where he could talk about his experiences and fears. I also think about Sarah, the scientist we met earlier who studies evolution and climate change. When she started learning more about evolution, she began to have some doubts about her faith. She told me what it was like to bring these doubts to her church community: "I grew up in a conflict model in the church. [When] I was interested in being in the sciences that was OK, until I started getting more interested in natural sciences and especially evolution, and I got the pressure that was pretty much like, 'Hey, you can either be a Christian or a scientist. You're going to have to choose.'"[14] Thankfully, Sarah did find a way to be both a Christian and a scientist, but how might her faith have been enhanced by a supportive Christian community?

Doubt in the midst of a faithful community is not necessarily damaging; it can lead to opportunities for growth and progress. Christian communities can embrace doubt as a powerful and useful tool for probing our faith and for asking hard questions that will test and prove the mettle of our faith. The doubts raised by science don't have to drive Christians away from faith; in my experience—as well as in the experience of many in my studies—doubts, if wrestled with prudently and productively in our churches and Christian communities, have the potential to hone and enhance our faith.

A Christian community I happened into during my undergraduate years at Cornell University brought me back to faith and into a local church different from the one I left. In the arms of its safe confines my doubts were held in the open, and over time my faith deepened. And just so, Jesus visited Thomas again, in compassion letting him see. The writer of the Gospel of John tells us that "a week later [Jesus's] disciples were in the house again, and Thomas was with them. Though the doors were locked, Jesus came and stood among them and said, 'Peace be with you!'" (John 20:26). Then Jesus spoke to Thomas specifically, addressing his doubts: "Put your finger here; see my hands. Reach out your hand and put it into my side. Stop doubting and believe" (20:27). And Thomas responded with awe, "My Lord and my God!" (20:28).

I believe that we should look at the scientific virtue of doubt as a religious virtue as well. Christian communities should become places where doubt is honored. Rather than something to be feared, *prudent doubt* can be a pathway to greater creativity and awe. As the writer Anne Lamott says, "To paraphrase Paul Tillich, the opposite of faith is not doubt, but certainty."[15]

And certainty may be missing the point entirely, forgetting that God is God and we are not. Faith, though, includes truthful recognition of the mess, the emptiness, the discomfort with what is unknown. It means holding them all in the safety of community and letting them be there until some light returns.

Further Discussion

1. Share one time when you felt doubt about your faith.
2. To what extent did you resolve that doubt?
3. Has science influenced or led to any doubts you have about your faith? If so, have you discussed these doubts with anyone? Would you feel comfortable discussing them at church?
4. How could your church change in order to help congregants feel freer discussing their doubts?

6

Humility

FOR MANY OF US, myself included, practicing doubt as a virtue can lead to humility. For example, if you had asked me when I first started my research whether there are many ways of being a *religious* scientist, I would have said, "Of course." If you had asked me whether there were many ways of being an *atheist* scientist, I probably would have said, "Not really"—being an atheist of any sort is by definition not to believe in God, simple as that. I was so sure I was right. But, as a sociologist, I have learned to doubt my assumptions, especially the assumptions I have about characteristics of groups. My studies of scientists over the past fifteen years have shown me that there are many varieties of atheism among scientists, including spiritual atheists and religious atheists. Discovering this diversity is just one of the ways that my research has humbled me and changed my previous thinking about a topic.

Humility is recognizing the limitations of our own understanding, abilities, and perspectives. Humility is being aware that we are not God. Sometimes this happens the hard way.

Sometimes you think you are going to conquer time and what you wind up with is a big purple toe that conquers your attempt to be super productive. A few years ago, I had a foot problem in the form of an ingrown toenail. While embarrassing to admit, it doesn't sound like that big of a deal. But by the time I was seated in my doctor's office, my toe was swollen and I was in pain. The podiatrist walked in, took one look at the toe, and announced that it was infected and needed to be taken care of immediately. He told me I would need minor surgery, something called a toenail resection, which would ensure that the toenail would not cause further infection. He also told me I was in luck because he could fit me right in.

For a long time, I have been afraid of hospitals. I am also afraid of needles and blood. But when a doctor tells you that you have a serious problem and require surgery, even a minor one, you listen. I have years of experience with both medical issues and earning a PhD, but I know that I know less than a doctor when it comes to issues related to health and well-being. I recognize my limited knowledge. What I do not readily acknowledge is my limited time.

After my minor surgery, the doctor told me I should go home and put my foot up. What I didn't tell him was that I planned to go ahead with several hours of afternoon meetings, one with a major university leader. I wasn't going to let minor surgery stop me. I walked out the door with a slight limp. And because my foot was still somewhat numb, I did not feel it when my foot banged right into the exit door. I looked down to see that my beige bandage had turned completely red with blood. I went back into the doctor's office to ask for help. Unfortunately, the office had run out of beige bandages and all they had left was bright purple. The nurse wrapped it around my foot many times, a clear reminder that I needed to take care of it, take it slow, and take time to rest. Sometimes there are signs of our own limits—big purple toe signs, for example.

As Christians we are familiar with the theological idea of humility. Our faith reminds us that God is God and we are not, and that full truth can never be known because of our human limitations and our limited ability to know the mind of God. This is not to say that there is no truth but to say that, as human beings, "we don't yet see things clearly," as pastor and theologian Eugene Peterson says in The Message, his paraphrase of the Bible. He translates, "We're squinting in a fog, peering through a mist. But it won't be long before the weather clears and the sun shines bright! We'll see it all then, see it all as clearly as God sees us, knowing him directly just as he knows us!" (1 Cor. 13:12). In other words, it's only when we see God face to face that we will know all. On this earth, we are all constrained by our limited human knowledge.

Humility, especially intellectual humility, is also a key scientific virtue. In the study of scientific virtues conducted by philosopher Robert Pennock, he found that "humility to evidence," defined as the "willingness to abandon a preferred hypothesis when faced with conflicting results," was one of the ten most widely held values of science as named by elite scientists.[1] My studies have examined how scientists practice humility in their pursuit of understanding and truth.

Humility in Science

"It gave me great pleasure to tell you about the mysteries with which physics confronts us," Albert Einstein once wrote in a letter to the queen of Belgium. "As a human being, one has been endowed with just enough intelligence to be able to see clearly how utterly inadequate that intelligence is when confronted with what exists. If such humility could be conveyed to everybody, the world of human activities would be more appealing."[2]

Scientists who practice intellectual humility are willing "to reconsider their views, to avoid defensiveness when challenged, and to moderate their own need to appear 'right.'" They "recognize and own their intellectual limitations in the service of pursuing deeper knowledge, truth, and understanding."[3] In other words, they acknowledge that while the tools of science help us understand the world and nature, human knowledge and understanding is limited. They hold their findings with an open hand, recognizing that they might be wrong. In the words of Subrahmanyan Chandrasekhar, a Nobel Prize–winning physicist, "Nature has shown over and over again that the kinds of truth which underlie nature transcend the most powerful minds."[4]

Writing about science and humility, Connor Wood, a research associate at the Center for Mind and Culture in Boston who has a doctorate in religion and science, says:

> I think science gives us remarkable tools to reflect on the world and come up with ways to test our ideas about it. But our ideas are always just that—our ideas. The world is, by definition, always bigger, badder, wilder, and more complex than our ideas could ever be. . . . You have to simplify the world to create models of it. [This] doesn't mean our models or ideas aren't accurate, or useful—not at all! . . . Just because science works doesn't mean it necessarily tells us the 100% truth about the world. And its success doesn't mean we shouldn't be humble—even radically humble. This goes for scientist and non-scientist, religious believer and skeptic. No matter how strong our convictions, we should always leave room for re-examining our beliefs, for being open to the unexpected. Otherwise our ideas about the world harden into stone—and stone is opaque.[5]

The Limits of Science

For many scientists who are Christians, humility in their work comes in part from the belief that they are trying to understand a universe created by God with laws and an order that make sense, even though they don't yet understand it all. "I was merely thinking God's thoughts after Him," mathematician and astronomer Johannes Kepler once said.[6]

People I interviewed expressed similar sentiments to those of Kepler. They often felt humbled by profound theological questions raised by science. While science can't know everything, the fact that humans, *as the limited creatures that we are*, can know anything at all about the universe was deeply meaningful. A Christian physicist told me, "The whole idea of being a scientist presupposes that the universe is understandable. That it's rational. And that is why I think one of my favorite quotes that I share with both believers and non-believers alike is from Albert Einstein, who said that the most incomprehensible thing about the universe is that it's comprehensible. And that was his basis . . . that especially those of us in areas like physics come face-to-face with. Why the universe is comprehensible."[7]

While humility is often lauded as a scientific virtue, Christians sometimes feel that nonreligious scientists have difficulty recognizing that science may be limited. Christians think that scientists are not open to the idea that there are other ways of pursuing knowledge and of understanding the world, particularly when it comes to the ethical implications of science: "It's very hard for a lot of scientists to remember that there are other ways of knowing things in the world, other than just the scientific framework . . . because you become so embedded within those practices," one biologist told me. "That frame of view [*pauses and sighs*] can be extremely challenging for faith."[8]

The Christians in science that I interviewed often talked about scientists who do *not* seem to practice intellectual humility, particularly in the way they interact with other Christians. But many in the scientific community also do not like scientists to act like they know it all. For example, in my work on how scientists respond to public intellectual Richard Dawkins, author of *The God Delusion*, I show how Dawkins is often perceived by his scientist critics as misrepresenting science and scientists. One cluster of UK scientists I interviewed said that they are not fans of how Dawkins talks about religion *or* science, feeling that, in arguing for the superiority of science over religion, his public engagement misrepresents what the process of science can do. One atheist biologist, discussing how to emphasize the limitations of science to students, told me, "Some people like Richard Dawkins. . . . He's a fundamental atheist. He feels compelled to take the evidence way beyond that which other scientists would regard as possible. . . . I want [students] to develop [science] in their own lives. And I think it's necessary to understand what science *does* address directly."[9]

A number of scientists my team and I interviewed believe that Dawkins, in particular, is not properly humble about science, betraying the scientific virtue of intellectual humility by not conveying the limits and limitations of scientific inquiry. Many atheist scientists think Dawkins gives the public the false impression that all scientists do—or should—share his kind of atheism. They also expressed concern that he makes it seem that scientists are dogmatic rather than open to new ideas. In their view, there are many atheist scientists who believe that questions related to meaning, purpose, or the existence of God are not inappropriate; these questions just fall outside the scope of science.

Here is where many atheist scientists and Christian scientists might actually agree. While they do not agree on the importance of faith, they may agree that science cannot explain everything. For example, a Christian biologist I interviewed said this: "I think we just accept that science is not a complete view of the world and so that means every scientific finding comes with an asterisk that . . . what we've come to is the best account of the world, you know, without considering God's action. If we consider God's action, that there's a theologically or scripturally motivated way to think about God's action, then maybe that would change our answer because science is only an incomplete view of the world."[10]

And in one survey I conducted, I found that about 31 percent of those in the general US population and 50 percent of evangelical Protestants *do not* think that, given enough time, science will be able to provide a natural explanation for everything. Only 16 percent of evangelical Christians in science and 23 percent of mainline Protestants in science *agree* that science will provide a complete natural explanation for our world.[11] It is important for those in churches to understand that the majority of scientists, Christian and non-Christian, take a humble approach to science.

Relational Humility

A few years ago, I read an article by Amanda King, an MD/PhD student. In it, she described how she was approached by other physicians and researchers to discuss a potential collaboration around her thesis project. "About two hours into the meeting, I realized that I was the only person in this room without at least one doctoral degree," she writes. "Yet these incredible scientists with decades of experience had been treating me—a second-year grad student—as an equal. . . . There was no reason why I should have been placed anywhere close to the same level. . . . So why were they treating me with such unearned respect?" King goes on to reflect, "Humility does not mean meekness. Humility does not mean unconditional deference. Humility does not mean *not* standing up for what you believe in—including when you believe in your own scientific findings. Humility means being open to the possibility of being wrong, being willing to consider other people's ideas and being respectful—of your seniors, your peers and your subordinates."[12]

From my own studies and experiences in science, I have seen that intellectual humility and hospitality as well as relational humility—embodying kindness and respect for the ideas of others no matter their status—go hand in hand. When we recognize that we are limited in our *own* understanding, abilities, and perspectives, we are humble and kind about the limitations of others. I have also noticed that practicing relational humility is not always easy for scientists, myself included. Science can be an extremely competitive environment that, as one scientist told me, "often seems to chew up and spit out individuals with little regard for human dignity."[13] Scientists often work incredibly long hours with no guarantee of payoff. Often, we get so caught up in our careers that we can forget the community of people who we are engaging with every day and who deserve to be treated with respect. We can also become too concerned with institutional status and prestige. Yet I have also found that many scientists place great importance on practicing relational humility in the workplace.

I have been thinking a lot lately about *practices* of intellectual and relational humility. One way I try to practice relational humility in my own work is through the Religion and Public Life Program, which I direct at Rice University. I, and the other leaders of the program, want to intentionally subvert the unending competition, the worship of status and prestige so common in elite academic environments. We try to practice relational humility by intentionally creating an environment of collaboration that seeks regular input from every member of the team, including undergraduates, graduate students, postdoctoral fellows, and full-time staff. To this end, once each week every member of the team gathers around a table and has the chance to offer ideas and feedback. We also use this time to celebrate each other's successes.

I found a special emphasis on relational humility among the scientists I interviewed who are Christian. Several of the Christian scientists I spoke with told me that caring for those they work with and mentor is extremely important to them.

They also said it was important to ensure that those around them are being treated with care and respect. They view their coworkers and students as people who are created in the image of God.

One evangelical Christian biologist recounted how he tried to use humility to shift the organizational culture of his work environment. He wanted to make sure that "there's a greater awareness that science is more than just [a set of ideas and methods]. It's more than just a career. It's more than just a method. It's a community of people that Jesus loves."[14] Another scientist explained how "her moral commitments as a Christian influence how she treats others," regardless of their rank or background. She explained, "As a Christian . . . I believe that people are equal and that everybody has the potential for good that makes them intrinsically valued, [which is] a very Christian belief."[15]

One biologist told me he felt that some of his colleagues were intensely competitive and had forgotten the quality of humility. He explained that the humility he brings to the workplace stems from his faith, allowing him to feel secure in his work and abilities and to expand his knowledge by interacting with the community of scientists around him without reservations. His sense of contentedness, he explained, "was generated from his understanding of the Christian faith and freed him to develop genuine relationships, including with potential competitors." His faith, he said, "always influences" how he treats his students. "I have tried to live my life helping people as much as I can. That includes my students," he said. "Their success is my success. And I think my upbringing [as a Christian] obviously influences that."[16]

While many nonreligious scientists demonstrate relational humility, treating their colleagues and students with respect and taking the time to encourage them, care for them, and learn from them (I want to make it clear that I have experienced deep care from my own academic colleagues who profess no particular faith), I found that Christian scientists tend to articulate faith-based reasons for a humble approach in their relationships with colleagues and students. In other words, many Christian scientists display a specific kind of relational humility in the workplace that they derive from their faith. They turn what to them is a Christian virtue into a scientific virtue also.

Some Christian scientists also discussed how important it is for scientists to treat the public with humility and respect, including religious believers. One Christian scientist, for example, described how she tries to share her scientific work with people of faith who are outside the science community in a way that is both understandable and respectful. As she explained,

> I can look at [natural principles] and just experience this amazing awe-piece that I was actually able to kind of put a name on, which I was like, wow, God did this, but look how cool these intricacies of how he made it work are. And so, for me, that gave that piece extra meaning. . . . Being able to share that with people in a way that is friendly to their religious predispositions is very important to me. I want the scientific message to be palatable, you know, and meet them where they're at.[17]

Displaying this kind of relational and intellectual humility can only improve the relationship between scientific and faith communities. When scientists exercise humility in regard to the beliefs of faith communities, they have the opportunity to teach these communities, even if disagreement exists. And when religious people exercise humility toward scientists, they have an opportunity to learn more deeply how God creates and sustains life, even if that is not the exact language scientists use.

Miracles

Nearly half the evangelical Christians I interviewed "affirmed their belief in the miracles of the Bible."[18] And when I surveyed evangelical Christians, in particular, about personal miraculous experiences, more than 39 percent reported witnessing a "miraculous, physical healing," and more than 23 percent reported experiencing one themselves.[19] For some Christians, believing in miracles is one way they practice humility. They remain open to the idea that there are events, phenomena, and healings that only God could create or explain.

But most scientists do not believe in miracles. In fact, only 36 percent of rank-and-file scientists agree to some degree that scientists should be open to considering miracles in their theories and explanations.[20] This belief is even less common among scientists who work in research universities. While, as we've seen, the majority of scientists take a humble approach to science—they do not believe that science will one day be able to provide a natural explanation for everything—the vast majority of scientists are also unwilling to consider or credit miracles for what we cannot yet explain or understand by natural causes. One evangelical Christian scientist I spoke with inhaled deeply and said, "I guess as a scientist I say, 'Well, there are things in the past that we couldn't explain that we can explain today.' And we say, 'Oh, now we know that the Northern Lights are not the hand of God directly . . . on the atmosphere. But no, they are the way that the sun's light is reflected through the atmosphere at this . . . longitude and latitude and so forth.'"[21] Thus even evangelical scientists demonstrate difficulty in acknowledging the existence of miracles.

At the same time, studies show that some Christian scientists do allow for the possibility of miracles. In fact, 55 percent of evangelical Christian rank-and-file scientists agree to some extent that scientists should be open to considering miracles in their theories and explanations.[22] "What I do think is that, you know, there's always the thing that occurs that you just never could have foreseen," a Christian physician told me. He said, "It kind of defies the natural history of the disease, if you will, or the process you would have been able to predict. . . . And the outcome's like 99 percent it should have been this, but it happened, that happened. And so that's challenging. . . . So the patient who is never supposed to survive—you know, metastatic disease, this is an experimental therapy, we're not sure it's going to work, and they're cured. That's a miracle!"[23]

A professor of physics I interviewed said, "I believe that miracles of all scales, including very small ones, happen, but that they happen as a way of God serving—or God being at work in the world—through, you know, in a way that communicates something to us." But she also believes such miracles are rare. She asked, "One miracle each day compared to all the things that happen according to the natural, normal functioning of the creation, that's a small amount, right?" She believes "that God created our universe with a rich, ordered structure to it" and that while God has complete control over the laws of nature, most of the time God "respects the kind of integrity of the creation," allowing the world to function as expected by natural law. When things occur that science cannot explain and appear to be miracles, she sees them as a direct act of God. "It's not just sort of random—God just sort of showing off, 'Oh, I can make the universe function not according to law,'" she said, "but it's for events that carry significance."[24] I remember the words of James, a Christian physicist who told me, "In the end, I need science, from my perspective as a scientist, to then make me understand that the scientifically impossible makes Jesus Christ's resurrection so extraordinary and substantiates his claim that he is the Son of God and that he died for our sins and is resurrected just as we have hope in the resurrection."[25]

Sharing Humility

Humility can help foster constructive dialogue between scientists and Christians by helping both sides respect the other's beliefs and open their minds to learning something new from each other. One Christian biologist I interviewed said he felt the relationship between science and religion would improve if there were greater willingness to consider other viewpoints that may challenge previously held beliefs. "I think what's really going on is that there's so much anxiety in the church. . . . There's such a lack of confidence, frankly [*chuckles*], that anything that—that destabilizes it, including an authentic Christian who just thinks differently about something, becomes very dangerous for people—it's very emotional," he said.[26] A Christian professor of immunology described constructive discussions on the relationship between science and religion that he was able to have because of his humble approach. "You see people across this whole continuum—I'm sure you have as well—who, you know, they're comfortable with where they are; they don't feel threatened or challenged by discussing it," he said. He went on to tell me, "But they're also like, 'I've got beliefs. I'm willing to be open to change. I'm willing to dialogue. I'm willing to hear your opinion. I want to tell you mine. I want to challenge you. I want you to challenge me.' And so I've had those discussions with people who are atheists or agnostics, and they've actually been very, very gratifying."[27]

If we Christians hope for humility from scientists—regarding the limits of scientific knowledge and respect for other ways of knowing—we must begin by modeling humility ourselves, a virtue that is at the core of our faith. We, too, must respect beliefs that are different from our own, accept that some of our conclusions might be wrong, recognize that we are all imperfect in our knowledge, and embrace that there is much that science can offer faith and our understanding of the world without undermining our faith. By taking a humble approach, we can begin to build bridges between science and faith.

Further Discussion

1. How do you embrace a sense of humility in church, in your work, or in your interactions with others?
2. Think about a time in your life when you felt humbled. How did this change your views?
3. Imagine a nonreligious scientist coming to your church. How would you show them that you respect their beliefs? What would you ask them?

7

Creativity

Though I grew up in a church that could be considered fundamentalist, it was my grandmother, my primary caregiver, who in many ways formed my identity as a Christian woman. She was a closet feminist. When it came to what my faith community considered the proper role for a woman (being a good wife and mother), she engaged in significant deprogramming efforts. "See this suit?" our pastor said during one of his sermons. "I have received a lot of compliments on it today. My wife made it for me." My grandmother pursed her lips. After we got home, she paced around, loudly announcing that I was going to get as much education as possible and was never going to sew for any man. Education, she believed, would protect me from dependency on a husband or an identity solely based on being a mother. It would also allow me to freely explore my creativity.

Many of the Christian scientists I have interviewed tell me that science itself is evidence of God's creativity. "I sort of feel like God kind of has a sense of humor with how there's so much in the creation that is surprising and delightful, and not just . . . solemn, and so I find a lot of that in seeing the various ways that quantum mechanics pops up in different parts," a physicist said.[1] And humans seem wired for that creativity. "There is little that shapes the human experience as profoundly and pervasively as creativity. Creativity drives progress in every human endeavor, from the arts to the sciences, business, and technology," writes psychologist Scott Barry Kaufman in an essay for *Scientific American*.[2] Creativity, some would say, is even *the* key way that humans are made in the image of God. According to Dorothy Sayers, when we look at a person we see "something divine, but when we turn back to see what [the person] says about the original upon which the 'image' of God was modeled, we find only the single assertion 'God created.' The characteristic [common] to God and to [humans] is apparently that: the desire and the ability to make things."[3] Biochemist and Anglican priest Robert Gilbert writes about science and play: "The playfulness of scientists is very good for the effectiveness with which [we] humans get a realistic understanding of reality. After all, the first and most fundamental characteristic of play is that it is free, that it operates freely."[4]

Although my grandmother feared that I might spend my days sewing, I never did learn to sew. I tried once to take a class but quickly decided that I was not meant to express my creativity in that way; it did not feel like play to me. But I do have three academic degrees, including a doctorate, and a meaningful career. I have had the privilege of being able to live creatively, to make things; my scientific work—research, teaching, writing, and mentoring—has allowed me the creative freedom to help others in ways I never could have imagined when I was a child. And at times it even feels like creative play to me.

Yet, after obtaining my degrees and beginning my career, I still desperately wanted to be a mother. In Christian communities, human life is seen as special and sacred, and children are seen as evidence of that specialness. Creating children, a family, and a home is talked about overtly or lifted up symbolically as an essential piece of being a good Christian and a good Christian *woman* in particular. In the beginning God created us, Christians believe, and then God empowered us to be creators, to "be fruitful and increase in number" (Gen. 1:28). In a number of churches, motherhood and mothering is elevated over all other kinds of creation or creativity.

My mother had eight children, and since fertility experts will tell you that one predictor of your ability to have children is the fertility of your mother, I felt certain that getting pregnant would not be a problem. If I wanted a baby, then I would have a baby. From everything I could see, babies just happened. I figured pregnancy would come easily to me as well, but it didn't. After more than fifteen years of trying to get pregnant and one significant pregnancy loss, I finally had a beautiful daughter, my only child.

Given the church's focus on children, family, and motherhood, Christians who do not have children, are not part of a nuclear family, or do not stay home with their children full time can feel judged at church, as if they are not entirely fulfilling their creative role. Jaime, one of the scientists we met before, told me, "Even though I am a scientist, my primary identity in church is as a mother. I come to church. I bring my daughter. My daughter is very good; she is extremely well-behaved in church. And so I feel as if we tick all of the socially appropriate women-in-the-church buttons, and it's *that* and not my scientific work that is absolutely my primary identity at church."[5]

In many church environments, having children and creating a family is considered the "norm." Yet for some, having children does not feel like part of their Christian calling; they feel called to other creative pursuits. For others, me included, their bodies do not function the way they would like them to, which means that even when they desperately want to have children, their biology does not cooperate.

About a year ago, I remember talking to a pastor I respect a great deal. In the course of our conversation about our work and our families, it came up that I have one child. "So you let your work get the best of you, didn't you?" he said. "So many women work so hard and then when they get near middle age they wish they had more children." I am not sure what compelled me toward honesty in that moment, but I replied, "Actually, I have been trying to get pregnant for the last fifteen years—the entire time I have been married—but have struggled deeply with infertility." He responded sheepishly that he was sorry. He also said that in his thirty years of ministry, he had not known very many people who spoke openly about infertility.

It would be helpful if churches became more willing to openly discuss infertility and its associated hardships with congregants so that the church can become a place of support and sympathy for those struggling to have children. Christians dealing with infertility often feel afraid to talk about their difficulty and despair with fellow congregants or to turn to their pastors for support. They suffer in silence. They believe they are the only ones experiencing the pain of infertility.

One Christian couple described how it felt to struggle with infertility in their faith community: "We soon discovered a gaping hole in the churches that we went to. With the exception of a few supportive Christians, people generally didn't talk about this problem unless we initiated it. There didn't seem to be many younger Christians who had thought about how to minister to people with infertility, and there didn't seem to be many older Christians who talked about their experience with it. The result was that people didn't know what to say to us."[6]

"My wife and I attend a church full of young families where people seem to have children all the time," explained Jeff Cavanaugh, a Christian writer who has chronicled how he and his wife have struggled with infertility. "Not only does such a church [environment] remind infertile couples of their infertility with painful regularity, it can also leave them feeling isolated and alone, out of step with everyone else their age in a different stage of life."[7]

In numerous ways, the Bible and church teachings tell us that children are a blessing from the Lord. The Old Testament psalmist, for example, writes,

> Children are a heritage from the Lord,
> offspring a reward from him.
> . . . .
> Blessed is the man
> whose quiver is full of them. (Ps. 127:3–5)

The cover of my first Bible depicted Jesus with little children flocking around him. I remember one woman in my church exclaiming when she was pregnant with her tenth child, "I cannot believe God has blessed me with another!" I have heard many times from people in churches that I have been part of, "I am praying for God to bless you with children." Because fertility is seen as a blessing, as the main or only way we can truly "create," those who do not or cannot have biological children can feel devalued, marginalized, and lonely. Phillip Wheeler, a pastor, explains that in the Scriptures "there is an expectation, even a command, to *be fruitful and multiply* and fill the earth, as part of a mandate given to [humanity]. There is an expectation that from a marriage union will come children."[8]

Wheeler also discusses how the stories of infertility in the Bible can be discouraging for Christian couples experiencing difficulty in having children. He explains, "The Bible is full of stories of women who were infertile and who experienced the pain of childlessness. Look at Sarah, or Rebekah, or Rachel and how distressed she became at the taunts of her rival, or Samson's mother, or Hannah or Elizabeth. In each of these cases, the woman was eventually able to conceive and give birth, for nothing is impossible with God."[9] Christians should try to reframe the narrative around infertility. The narrative should not be limited to stories of hope that result in God bringing biological children but should include both stories of hope *and* stories of suffering. Questioning, doubts, worry, and even dissatisfaction with a life different from the one a believer had wished for can often lead to glorifying God.

"Fertility is described in the Bible as a blessing for the obedient and infertility as a curse from God," writes Megan Best, a Christian doctor and bioethicist, in an article for the Gospel Coalition. "Some couples, then, may need reassurance that while all the sickness, suffering, and trouble of our world results from the fall, problems like infertility aren't necessarily connected with our personal sins in a neat one-to-one correspondence."[10]

In an article she wrote for *Time* magazine on how the church could show more compassion for those facing infertility, Elizabeth Hagan, a Christian pastor who struggled with infertility herself for eight years before adopting, wrote that she "often wondered: If I wasn't the pastor, would I come to church during this difficult time? The answer on many occasions was no." She said that Christian leaders do not often provide words of comfort or encouragement to those struggling with infertility and that couples do not feel safe discussing at church their struggle with infertility. Part of the problem, she writes, is that "with the idea of immaculate conception sitting center stage every December, the church is a sucker for a good miracle story. It's not that miracle babies aren't possible. . . . But not every couple gets a miracle. Instead of focusing on the few miracles that do occur, the church needs to highlight stories of resilience. For example, the woman who still gets out of bed in the morning after her in-vitro fertilization cycle didn't work." For Hagan, "the bottom line is that the church would be wise to learn that infertility is a medical condition, not a spiritual one."[11]

Fertility, Faith, and Science

Today, more and more Christians who struggle with infertility are turning to science (alongside or as part of their faith) to seek help with conceiving. The existence of these technologies is a piece of scientists' own creative pursuits to alleviate the suffering of infertility. In-vitro fertilization (IVF) is the most common and effective type of assisted reproductive technology that is used to treat infertility. During IVF, a woman's eggs are removed from her body and mixed with sperm to form embryos (the early form of the egg and sperm after they have just joined), which are then implanted back in the woman's body. Assisted reproductive technologies sometimes use eggs or sperm from donors, or they use previously frozen embryos. They may also involve a surrogate or gestational carrier. A surrogate provides her own eggs, while a gestational carrier "becomes pregnant with an egg from the female partner and the sperm from the male partner."[12]

These technologies are not without their problems. Assisted reproductive technologies are typically not covered by insurance and can be extremely costly—an IVF cycle can cost $15,000 or more, for example, which means it is often available only to the wealthy.[13] I spent thousands of dollars on fertility treatments. In churches, the fact that one is even using infertility technologies feels like it should be kept secret. Although I talked with close friends at work about my infertility and treatments, I almost never talked about these things at church. Fertility technologies also do not seem accessible to all. (During the entire time period that I went to an infertility clinic, I only saw a handful of nonwhite couples in the office waiting area, which is remarkable given that I live in the most racially and ethnically diverse city in the US.)

These technologies are nonetheless becoming more and more common. And, for many, these technologies seem like a sign of the God-given creative capacity humans have. Between 1987 and 2015, more than one million babies born in the US were conceived through the use of IVF or other assisted reproductive technologies, according to a report released in 2017 by the US Society of Assisted Reproductive Technology.[14] Most churches, whether or not the leadership or congregants are aware, likely have kids running around who were born through the help of assisted reproductive technologies like IVF.

When it comes to creating new technologies that seem to construct the beginning of life, some Christians raise moral concerns about whether such technologies represent imprudent or unfettered creativity. My research shows that Christians tend to have complex feelings about assisted reproductive technologies. On the one hand, they see the benefits these technologies can afford. By helping couples dealing with infertility, these technologies have the potential to alleviate suffering. They can also help bring children into the world and church. On the other hand, there are concerns that these technologies allow scientists to "play God" and interfere with God's will. Some Christians believe children are a blessing that should come only naturally, directly "from God and not from a test tube," as I have heard some in churches say. And the process of IVF generally results in the creation of more embryos than can be used. Some are kept frozen and some are donated to other couples, but some of the embryos are destroyed in research or other parts of the process, and a large minority of Christians see this as destroying human life. "The procedures have amplified profound questions for the world's theologians," reporter Ariana Eunjung Cha wrote in a *Washington Post* article on the fortieth anniversary of the birth of the first IVF baby. She continued, vocalizing these questions: "When does life begin? If it begins at conception, is it a sin to destroy a fertilized egg? What defines a parent? Is the mother the woman who provides the egg or the woman who gives birth? What defines a marriage? If a man's sperm fertilizes an egg from a woman who is not his wife, does that constitute adultery?"[15]

As Christians face these and other questions related to technologies that treat infertility, they often have to decide between competing theological ideals. For evangelical Christians, sources of authority for the faith, such as the Bible and Christian doctrines, are central in shaping how they weigh the potential benefits of these technologies against the importance of protecting embryos and the sacredness of life. In a national survey I conducted, I found that evangelical Christians are more likely than members of other major faith traditions to express moral concerns about IVF. Of evangelicals who were surveyed, 18 percent identified IVF as "morally objectionable" compared with 13 percent of all Americans, 15 percent of Catholics, and 11 percent of Protestants more broadly.[16]

Concerns about humans "playing God" or usurping God's creative role often came up in discussions about IVF with Christians who find it morally objectionable. Some Christians believe that "unnatural" intervention in the process of conceiving children diminishes the role of God because it allows humans to involve themselves in the process of creation. They see assisted reproductive technologies as interfering with what is "meant to be." As one evangelical woman opined, "It's not the right thing to do. [Those who use IVF] are treading on places that can get very dangerous—the word *dangerous* may not be right—but it could become disastrous. . . . I believe people who cannot have children need to resolve the fact that they do not. And they need to find children they can adopt, or they can love the children they encounter in life. That's probably what is meant for them to do."[17] This woman views infertility as at least a temporarily immutable imposition from God that should not be changed but that should cause those who do suffer from infertility to love children already in the world who need love.

One Christian couple recalled a friend who, upon learning they were undergoing IVF, told them, "I really think you should be adopting instead; it's much more ethical." The friend did end up apologizing, but the initial response reflects a commonly held position in the church. Christians who support or undergo IVF often experience backlash from their fellow Christians and congregants. In one church service I attended, we had a rare discussion group on fertility technologies. One woman raised her hand with tears in her eyes to say this was the first time she felt freedom to say that her children were conceived through the support of IVF technologies; she wanted to share this with the congregation so that others who are struggling with infertility might have someone to talk with.[18]

Yet I have also found that many evangelical Christians do not have moral objections to IVF. Among the evangelical Christians I surveyed, 42 percent say IVF is always morally acceptable or is morally acceptable in most cases, and another 32 percent say it is not a moral issue.[19] Many of them believe that God affords humans the ability to create and advance medical technologies, and because God actively allows humans to discover and use these technologies, they do not see these technologies as replacing the role of God. Instead, God is, in a way, working through these technologies and through the creative power he gives to the humans who created them and to the humans who use them. Put another way, these Christians view technologies like IVF as God-given tools that allow humans to work in partnership with God. I call this moral framework a "co-creator schema" (in which humans, through the gifts of God, share the creator role).

Christians offer many reasons for their support of IVF technologies. One woman I interviewed at a church in Houston explained, "I do not believe that [IVF] in any way goes against the fact that God created the egg and the sperm. . . . He just made people smarter to where they can harvest them and freeze them and use them. No, I do not have a problem with that!"[20] Another evangelical Christian explained that IVF could be part of humans and God working together. For him, IVF is "one of those things God has revealed science to do to help people," and thus scientists and God are seen as working together.[21] A Christian biologist I interviewed talked about how a couple in his church applied their Christian principles to how they used IVF:

> I [knew] one couple who . . . knew that the standard practice, which is still pretty prevalent, is that they would do what's called hyper-ovulation or super-ovulation where you would get many oocytes [eggs] produced by the woman and then [the fertility doctors] would fertilize all of them, but not implant all of the fertilized embryos. And then the rest are frozen. And [the couple wasn't] comfortable with those embryos sitting in a freezer in liquid nitrogen some place for years. So they wanted to go to an IVF clinic where they would only fertilize enough oocytes that they could implant all of them if they all successfully developed. So that's one specific way that [someone's faith matters]. They are pretty savvy, that couple, I will say. I mean they thought about a lot.[22]

Future Humans

Like assisted reproductive technologies, gene-editing technologies, which allow scientists to change the genetic makeup of a fertilized egg by inserting, deleting, or modifying DNA, also trouble some Christians because of ethical concerns and feelings they have about the creative power of God and the sacredness of human life. A 2016 survey by the Pew Research Center revealed that "highly religious Americans are much more likely than those who are less religious to say they would not want to use gene-editing technology in their families."[23] According to Pew, many Christians felt that using gene editing to reduce the risk of disease in babies was morally *un*acceptable. They were concerned that it would be altering "God's plan" or "going against nature."[24] Among Protestants overall, 54 percent see gene editing that would reduce the risk of serious diseases in babies as meddling with nature, compared with 31 percent of those who have no religious affiliation. (Among white evangelical Protestants, the number goes up to 61 percent, while 42 percent of white mainline Protestants and 50 percent of black Protestants felt the same.) Those who felt gene editing for this purpose was morally acceptable referenced its similarity to other medical advances and pointed to the potential positive effects.[25]

My research has found that most evangelical Christians support the use of disease-focused reproductive genetic technologies (RGTs for short)—that is, gene editing and genetic testing technologies that focus primarily on correcting diseases or health concerns in embryos in the womb. Only 23 percent of evangelical Christians view disease-focused RGTs as morally wrong. Evangelicals who feel these are wrong often think that using these technologies inserts humans into the process of creation, debasing human life, interfering with God's plan, or contesting God's role as creator. For example, one young evangelical man who works in medicine told me, "I believe God is in control and that he's taking care of everything, and [if] this child has a disease, then that's what God wants for this child."[26] Even though the detection of developmental maladies in utero is a routine part of prenatal care in the US and even though medical professionals typically neither need nor use genetic testing to do it, many Christians worry that disease-focused RGTs will lead to a greater number of abortions. They reason that if the unborn child cannot be "fixed," then it will be aborted.

Evangelicals who express support for disease-focused RGTs often do so based on the "co-creator schema" discussed earlier. They believe God provides humans with the knowledge and guidance to discover medical technologies, and thus God is working through these technologies and the humans who use them. I interviewed one woman from Houston who says, "I feel that they [scientists] have research that finds illnesses and sicknesses or corrective surgery that could be done while the baby is still in the womb; I think that is fantastic!"[27] A youth minister in one evangelical church recounted a personal experience that altered his views toward disease-focused RGTs. He learned his child might have Trisomy 18, a chromosomal disorder that often results in death shortly after birth. While his child did not end up having the condition, he said that he would have used genetic technologies had they been able to prevent his child's condition and that he was now open to using disease-focused RGTs to treat an ailment before birth. Drawing on "co-creator" beliefs, he explained, "If God's giving me the power and the ability and the know-how to do it, I'd do it."[28] One of the most interesting findings from my research on how evangelical Christians view these technologies is that their feelings are not always static and their attitudes toward the moral permissibility of these technologies can be changed by personal experiences.

I have also looked at how Christians feel about enhancement RGTs. These RGTs are used not to identify and treat diseases in embryos but rather to select or create specific characteristics in an embryo, like athleticism or eye color, for perceived enhancement purposes.[29] Many of these technologies are not yet possible, but many people, including most Christians, are concerned about what enhancement RGTs might lead to. When my colleagues and I spoke with evangelicals, most of them expressed views on enhancement RGTs that are similar to the views of the general American population, raising moral concerns about these potential technologies. In one survey I conducted, 80 percent of evangelical Christians indicated that they saw enhancement RGTs as morally wrong. Evangelical Christians often believed these technologies lead to "playing God" or usurping God's creative power. For example, one man from an evangelical congregation in Houston said, "I referenced the Tower of Babel a little earlier and people tried to build a tower so high that they could get to God, that they could be equal with God. . . . And I think when we start playing God with human genetics, we are doing the same thing. We're putting ourselves equal with God, so . . . I think that would be sinful."[30]

Most of the time, however, when I questioned evangelicals about enhancement RGTs, they could not articulate their feelings of discomfort or disapproval, nor could they provide a religious or moral framework to explain their feelings. Rather, these feelings, while present, were a visceral reaction. This technology simply did not feel right, but they did not have the language to say why.

Sometimes we have to wrestle with our technologies and newfound abilities. We have to make hard choices between theological ideals and competing values. We have to think about what the limits of scientific creativity should be, what technologies we should wield, how we can use them for good, and how they might go wrong. Beyond reproductive technologies, we have to think about our responsibilities to all we create and to everything we bring into this world. One part of exercising responsibility with our God-given creative power is using it for redemptive healing.

Further Discussion

1. If you feel comfortable sharing, have you ever struggled with infertility or known someone who has?
2. What could your church do to help congregants feel more comfortable opening up about issues related to fertility?

3. What are your thoughts on the "co-creator schema"? Does it help you envision different ways of seeing God's creator role and of honoring the specialness of human life? Are there other ways you think reproductive technologies can be reconciled with your faith?
4. How can your congregation better nurture the creative capacity of its members?

PART 3

REDEMPTION

8

Healing

"You should hear what they say about you." We were sitting around the dinner table and Anika was telling us that some kids had been picking on her about her parents. "Do you want to know what they say about you, Daddy?" Karl said he wasn't sure, but she persisted. "They say, 'Your dad has gray hair. Is he your grandfather?'" We talked about this for a bit, and then she turned to me: "You should hear what they say about you, Mommy."

"Oh. What do they say?" I replied, trying to sound nonchalant, while my heart was secretly racing at the thought of what might come next. "They say, 'Your mom's hands look really weird. Does she have something wrong with her?'" Her words brought noticeable tears to my eyes.

Most days for the past thirty years I have experienced at least some pain in my hands, a result of joint degeneration from rheumatoid arthritis. In high school, there were times I sat on my hands so others would not notice when they turned blue at the slightest bit of cold. On my wedding day, I wore long gloves because I did not want to think about my hands. I have largely dealt with these emotions, and now I very rarely feel like I need to hide my hands or improve their appearance through reconstructive surgery, a procedure I have at times considered. But thinking of other kids teasing my daughter because of *my* hands brought some of those old feelings back. My hands have caused physical and emotional suffering—though I know that my suffering, while significant to me, has been small compared with the suffering of so many others. Medicine and doctors have also been able to alleviate some of my suffering.

When my daughter was three years old and I had just started leading a big international research study, my orthopedic surgeon told me the cartilage in my hip joint had been completely worn away. Every step I took with my thirty-eight-year-old body wracked me with pain. "You must be suffering. I think I can get you in for surgery next week," my doctor said after looking at my X-rays. "How will I take care of a three-year-old while I am recovering from a hip replacement? And how will I continue with my work?" I asked. He looked at me and replied in a soft voice, "You need to ask yourself, will you be able to take care of your three-year-old and do your work from a wheelchair?" Four weeks later, I ambled slowly behind a walker—the kind you see being used by ninety-year-olds in nursing homes—and into my classroom to teach. Eight weeks after my surgery, I sent my doctor a picture of me hiking in the hills of California. I have deep gratitude and respect for what is aptly called the "wonders of modern medicine"; without them, rheumatoid patients like me would not be able to walk.

My research shows that members of both scientific communities and religious communities place high value on alleviating the suffering of others. "Suffering is a great mystery, and human suffering is something that when it's in our power to alleviate, we should do so in my opinion," a Christian professor of biology told me. He believes using his research to alleviate suffering is part of his calling as a scientist.[1] Another evangelical biologist told me he sees scientific research and technology as "a way to intervene, to provide relief from suffering."[2]

However, how we offer healing (both the technologies we use to do so and when we should prioritize alleviating suffering above other core commitments and values) is an issue religious believers grapple with. Some Christians believe that in pursuing and using certain medical technologies to alleviate suffering, we sometimes become misguided. Some are concerned that scientists focus too heavily on using technology to reduce or eliminate the presence of suffering, sacrificing other important values. In their view, a life free of all suffering is not necessarily the ultimate goal. I have also found that there are some Christians who, based on their faith, think of suffering itself as inculcating other virtues, like empathy for those who suffer. "Christians affirm that there are resources for living in the midst of suffering that are unique . . . in the Christian tradition," one professor of biology told me.[3]

Reducing Suffering

Research has shown that many Christians appreciate medicine's ability to reduce physical suffering like mine. According to one national survey, Christians and non-Christians differ little in their degree of confidence in institutional medicine: 35 percent of Christians versus 38 percent of non-Christians said they had a great deal of confidence in medicine.[4] When I have compared Christians with other groups of people, I have found little difference in their affirmation of medical technologies and discoveries. I have also found that Christians are more affirming of medical research than they are of basic scientific research. I believe this is in part because medicine is perceived as more directly helping people and therefore perceived by some Christians as having greater potential for both healing and spiritual import.

A number of Christians I interviewed spoke positively about medical technologies as a way to alleviate suffering and offer healing. Christians often focus on lessening the suffering of others in order to bring God's peace to the world and to the human body. Much in the Bible supports this idea; a huge part of Jesus's ministry on earth involved touching those whom others would not touch, healing those whom others thought were beyond healing. Christians holding this theological view can see medical technologies as created by God for us to use to relieve our suffering and the suffering of others. One Christian I interviewed explained, "Medicine is a gift from God, and medicine was given to the doctors and the researchers to help God's people. [It is as if God is saying], 'I gave [the doctor] the medicine, and I made you, so I'm going to send you over there to get some help from the doctor, from the science, from the medicine that I have created for you.'"[5]

Another evangelical youth minister agreed with this sentiment. "For us, it's 'praise the Lord' that doctors have been given the knowledge to be able to come up with things like [cancer treatment technology]. . . . New technologies in X-ray and radiological scanning are phenomenal."[6] Such comments show an overall affirmation of technologies that seem to alleviate the suffering of others. And yet, not all Christians prioritize physical healing as the highest value.

Moral Risks in Alleviating Suffering

For some Christians, alleviating suffering should not come at any cost. For them, the virtue should be applied prudently, and we must decide when alleviating suffering should be our ultimate goal and when other virtues should take priority. "Is it a good goal for humans to physically flourish? Yes. And so Christians should seek to avoid human suffering where they can, absolutely," one Christian professor of biology (introduced earlier) explained. "However, I just detect in a lot of the rhetoric associated with the applications of medicine and human biotechnology that sometimes we've crossed the line into elevating our own physical well-being to be *the* chief good. Christians fundamentally identify the ultimate in human flourishing as living a blessed life. That is not the same as being healthy and the colloquial use of the word *happy*. . . . A blessed human life is a life lived in alignment with God's purposes for human life."[7]

In the last chapter, I introduced reproductive genetic technologies (RGTs), which allow scientists to acquire or alter genetic information in embryos. Disease-focused RGTs, which are used to screen embryos and sometimes to identify and treat disease in the womb, clearly have great capacity to reduce suffering, which is why some Christians support these technologies, even as they worry about their theological and ethical implications (namely, that these technologies diminish the sanctity of life and role of God).[8]

Sociologist John H. Evans suggests that Christians' views on RGTs are greatly influenced by whether they see suffering as something to be reduced or as having a possible redemptive benefit.[9] Most individuals view suffering in only a negative way and want to heal illness and disease as quickly as possible—or, better yet, prevent them altogether. Most Christians even support genetic means for alleviating suffering, and thus they express strong support for the use of disease-focused RGTs.[10] While Evans found that most of the evangelical Christians he surveyed expressed support for using RGTs to reduce suffering, many in the group also saw a potential value in suffering. Some Christians believe, for example, that suffering is part of God's plan or can serve a greater good and be part of a good life because it opens us up to greater empathy, compassion, and resilience and because it teaches us how to better comfort and support others in need.

In an essay for *The Conversation*, Evans also discusses how what is seen as a form of suffering can get fuzzy. "Once you figure out how to change one gene, you can change any gene, regardless of its function. If we fix sickle cell, why not deafness, or late onset heart disease, or a lack of 'normal' intelligence, or as we approach the bottom, a lack of superior intelligence?" he writes. He later adds, "We also cannot simply rely upon the medical profession to define disease, as some practitioners are engaged in activities that are more aptly described as enhancement (think plastic surgery). A recent report by the National Academy of Sciences concluded that the distinction between disease and enhancement is hopelessly muddled."[11]

Research using human embryonic stem cells (hESCs) that aims to alleviate disease raises many of the same theological and ethical issues for Christians as RGT use does. More specifically, it forces us as Christians to adjudicate between two important moral principles: the duty to respect the value of human life and the duty to prevent or alleviate suffering. Human embryonic stem cells are cells found in an embryo before it is implanted in the uterus.[12] These cells are special because they have the "ability to form cells ranging from muscle to nerve to blood," and thus they provide an "essentially unlimited supply of specific cell types for basic research."[13] Scientists can use these cells to research many diseases, including heart disease and leukemia, to name just a few. To obtain embryonic stem cells, the early embryo has to be destroyed. This means destroying a potential human life. But human embryonic stem cell research could lead to the discovery of new medical treatments that would alleviate the suffering of millions of people.[14] Herein lies the struggle for many Christians.

In a national survey I conducted with sociologist Christopher Scheitle, we found that about 66 percent of evangelicals said they believed the destruction of human embryos, even in the context of trying to cure diseases, is morally wrong.[15]

According to one of my studies, 44 percent of Christian scientists in the US strongly or somewhat agree that the government should support research that uses cells derived from lab-created human embryos (60 percent of all US scientists surveyed feel the same).[16] Some Christians (including some Christian scientists) who have reservations about the research explained their ultimate support for hESC research by accentuating its ability to reduce suffering and advance the greater good. Rebecca, a Christian neuropsychologist who holds such a view, explained it this way: "If the work is conducted in an ethical manner and with the purpose to benefit human life, I think it is OK. . . . Life begins at conception. However, if there's a situation where people do come into contact with [human] embryonic stem cells, then there might be redemption if they are used from the greater knowledge and the greater good as a result."[17]

Another Christian told me that, for her, the potential to heal far outweighs the potential moral complications of hESC research, and in her view, we have an imperative to conduct hESC research *because* life is sacred. She explained:

> [Human embryonic stem cells] can be absolutely any cell type in the body. You just have to give them the right signal. Which makes them incredibly powerful as a therapeutic technique. . . . People who've had spinal injury, potentially we could . . . repair some of their nerves and they could walk again. And people with pancreatic cancer, we could take out their pancreas and give them a new pancreas. . . . People's lives would be incredibly enriched by this technology. And it sounds counterintuitive, but life is sacred, right? And suffering is, suffering's not good. Nobody wishes suffering on anyone else. And there's ways to improve life.[18]

One Christian professor of genetics talked in a similar way about gene-editing technologies, which is the focus of his work.[19] He explained, "If it's such a clear thing, like this mutation will always cause this disease, then we can probably rally around that cause as well, right? And some might even say, as I would: Gosh, if you had the opportunity to do that, it would be more wrong not to." He does worry, however, that the technologies open up serious questions regarding economic inequality and racial injustice—other forms of suffering—meaning that researchers need to ask who will have access to potential treatments and for whom those treatments will be developed. Alleviating suffering now could lead to other forms of future suffering, which means medical technologies sometimes require Christians to weigh different and competing forms of suffering. An evangelical biologist agreed, saying that he "wants to do scientific work that improves the common good, but whatever advance I come up with could just as easily be used to create injustice in the world."[20]

Another form of gene editing is *human germline gene editing*, which is controversial because it changes a person's genome in such a way that the changes are passed down to subsequent generations. Among other concerns is the concern that such technology has the potential to introduce new forms of suffering. According to one scientist, "One of the biggest risks of germline editing therapy is the introduction of alleles with unforeseen side-effects that would be recognized generations after initial gene editing."[21] For some, this is the very definition of playing God.

Offering Comfort to Others

There is much biblical evidence of Christ suffering with the poor, the lonely, and the ill. What does it mean for us in our Christian communities to suffer with those who are ill? One of my studies took me into hospitals to talk with pediatric oncologists about how they view the relationship between faith and science. A few of the doctors I spoke with were atheists or agnostics, but many were Christians or members of another faith. I found that doctors who did not have personal faith often did have tremendous respect for the faith of their patients, and they saw a need for religious or spiritual care alongside medical care. One pediatric oncologist described her deep pain at seeing her patients suffer, and she said, "I'm probably more toward the agnostic end—in that for me I can't reconcile, you know, how do I say it, a God who would let a kid get stage-four neuroblastoma and die a painful death."[22]

Dave Zuleger, a Christian pastor, points out that in the New Testament (2 Cor. 1:11), Paul asks many to pray for him so that when God continues to grant Paul life, God will get more glory and be better known by others. Paul realizes that sharing his own suffering and burdens with others gives glory to God and highlights, in Zuleger's words, "God's powerful sustaining grace."[23] Paul offers a similar thought: "Blessed be the God and Father of our Lord Jesus Christ, the Father of mercies and God of all comfort, who comforts us in all our affliction, so that we may be able to comfort those who are in any affliction, with the comfort with which we ourselves are comforted by God. For as we share abundantly in Christ's sufferings, so through Christ we share abundantly in comfort too" (2 Cor. 1:3–5 ESV). Some interpret Paul's words here to mean that suffering with others is part of God's plan for us; God comforts *in suffering* so that we can then comfort others. Our suffering gives us the ability to offer others who are suffering genuine empathy and compassion.

Sue Bohlin, a Christian speaker, similarly describes her view that "suffering prepares us to minister comfort to others who suffer," helping grant them fortitude. She writes, "Your pain may not be just about you. It may well be about other people, preparing you to minister comfort and hope to someone in your future who will need what you can give them because of what you're going through right now."[24]

Some Christians likewise believe we can find meaning in suffering. They do not glorify suffering, but they do have hope that suffering might be used for a greater purpose. Some believe that by enduring personal suffering, we can act in service to others. One Christian professor of biology, who earlier spoke about the importance of reducing human suffering, said, "I do sense in some way that God in the very least can take the suffering that we as limited humans experience . . . and bring good out of it."[25] He continued, "So there can be redemptive outcomes of those sufferings. That doesn't mean I don't wish the sufferings weren't there. I do. But I also observe, at least in my own limited way, and I'm very limited, but I see in a much greater way and in the lives of other people who've undergone tremendous suffering, that God can bring good out of that." Such Christians maintain hope that in their suffering is the possibility for redemption.

"I'm suffering, but the cool thing is that my heart has been open to the suffering of this world," said Todd Neva, a Christian writer and quadriplegic living with ALS.[26] Todd and his wife, Kristin, use their faith to give their suffering meaning. "Anybody who's owned a car knows that the more features are on a car, the more can go wrong. And as such, in the most complex machine ever designed, one little glitch in the human body—one little protein missing, one little DNA chain broken, one bad chromosome, one little contamination—we have sickness, disease, and suffering," he writes in one post on his blog. "There's no possible way to know all that can go wrong, and there's no way to live a life completely free of risk. Sometimes things just happen," he later concludes.[27] Add to this Duke University professor Kate Bowler's beautiful and hard memoir on what it is like to be a young person and a Christian in the midst of a stage-four cancer diagnosis: "The horror of cancer has made everything seem like it is painted in bright colors. I think the same thoughts again and again: Life is so beautiful. Life is so hard." Bowler explains, "When they [people encouraging her] sat beside me, my hand in their hands, my own suffering began to feel like it had revealed to me the suffering of others."[28]

One evangelical biologist I interviewed discussed Martin Price as a personal role model. Price founded ECHO, a Christian organization that strives to "reduce hunger and improve lives worldwide."[29] In this biologist's view, Price could have done other things with his career, things that would have brought him more resources personally. But he sees Price as "a person who's been obedient unto suffering in the service of the common good and the service of the church and the service of lost people." The biologist explained that he wants "to do scientific work that improves the common good," but he does not believe that science can fix all the problems of the world. Thus the world needs people who are willing to suffer for the common good. "What is missing is people who are actually following Jesus's example, the obedience and the suffering, laying out the power they've been given in the service of people who by all accounts are not their family," he said.[30]

To return to the story I told at the beginning of this chapter, I think I experienced a little bit of Jesus's healing later that night, redemption of a different sort than that which has come through my doctors. When I was putting Anika to bed after dinner and her bath, she carefully put her hands over mine and stroked them softly. "I noticed your tears, and I am sorry I hurt your feelings," she said. "I want you to know that you do not need to get surgery to make your hands look better. I love your hands just the way they are because they are my mom's hands."

Further Discussion

1. What has been your experience of physical suffering? Have you ever shared or journaled about this suffering?

2. What has been your experience of caring for others who are physically suffering? Of helping others access the medical care they need?
3. What are your thoughts on reproductive genetic technologies? If you still have questions about the technologies and their implications, where can you go to find answers?
4. Think about a time when medicine helped someone close to you. How did you feel about this medical technology? How do you think about the relationship between medicine and your faith?
5. How do you think about the moral issues related to certain medical technologies? To what extent does your church community help you think through these issues?
6. Do you think we should do everything we can to eliminate suffering, or do you think there are other virtues or values we should prioritize over eliminating suffering?

9

Awe

SEVERAL YEARS AGO, Jennifer Wiseman, a Christian astrophysicist at NASA, came to my church to give a talk.[1] My husband introduced her: "I was reading Psalm 19 and I appreciate the verse that says, 'The Heavens declare the glories of God' [v. 1], but when Jennifer reads this, she sees so much more than I do," he said. "She has a much deeper sense of the awe that comes through witnessing the expansion of the stars through her work as an astronomer. And she is here with us tonight to bring us—the people in our church who are not scientists—a deeper sense of that awe."

Many scientists talk about how seeing the beauty of the natural world through their work fills them with a sense of wonder and awe, which they hold in high value. Dissecting, examining, and understanding the natural world—even its smallest, most intricate parts—only increase their feelings of astonishment, amazement, and appreciation. "First of all, the beauty that [the average person] sees is available to other people—and to me, too. . . . I can appreciate the beauty of a flower," said Richard

Feynman, one of the greatest physicists of our modern era. Feynman also knew that a deep curiosity could bring deep awe:

> At the same time, I see much more in the flower than he sees. I can imagine the cells inside, which also have a beauty. There's beauty not just at the dimension of one centimeter; there's also beauty at a smaller dimension.
>
> There are the complicated actions of the cells, and other processes. . . . All kinds of interesting questions that come from a knowledge of science, which only adds to the excitement and mystery and awe of a flower. It only adds. I don't understand how it subtracts.[2]

Even atheist scientists like Richard Dawkins describe feeling awed by science. "The feeling of awed wonder that science can give us is one of the highest experiences of which the human psyche is capable," he writes. "It is a deep aesthetic passion to rank with the finest that music and poetry can deliver."[3]

Awe is a virtue, connected perhaps most deeply to the virtues of humility and curiosity. Being "passionately curious," to quote Einstein, leads us on the search, and the end of that search is often awe.[4] Awe is a deep appreciation of the "other" and of the potential beauty and goodness of the "other." And awe flows, in part, from a deep acknowledgment of our own limitations. Possibly charting a path between humility and awe, Paul Piff (assistant professor of psychology and social behavior at the University of California, Irvine) and Dacher Keltner (professor of psychology at the University of California, Berkeley) explain that awe is "the feeling of being in the presence of something vast that transcends our understanding of the world."[5] And the philosopher Kristján Kristjánsson, a professor of character education and virtue ethics at the University of Birmingham, explains his own experience of awe this way:

> I first visited Hljóðaklettar—a well-known area of columnar-craters, presenting unique "basalt roses," in a national park

> in the north-east of Iceland—on an early October day as a seventeen-year-old. All the tourists had gone; there was not a single person in sight, only the "rosy" columns surrounded by low birch trees in autumn colors, with a mighty grey glacial river providing a stark background contrast. I experienced feelings of aesthetic ecstasy, mingled with a sense of enormity, oneness, and of time standing still. I have never been fully able to recapture that feeling, there or elsewhere although I have caught glimpses of it when listening to great pieces of music such as Tchaikovsky's Violin Concerto.[6]

For Kristjánsson the deepest sense of awe—like it is for many of the scientists I interviewed—can feel like a once-in-a-lifetime experience. The natural world and scientific explorations of nature can elicit an awe akin to the awe solicited by God, and scientists who are Christians (those who have a foot in both communities) may show us how scientific awe and religious awe may be one and the same.

Discovering Awe in Science

Many Christian scientists talked to me about seeing beauty in nature and about the feelings of awe and wonder that nature evokes. For some, this fascination with nature is a huge part of why they do science. One Christian physicist described feeling "awe and wonder at nature in general." He said, "I feel like there's no point doing science if you don't feel that. Why go into this low-paying, high-stress field . . . if you don't think that there's something amazing about nature and that it's a fun and interesting thing to study? . . . I can't imagine *not* having that feeling, I guess," he concluded.[7] A Christian biologist expressed similar feelings: "We're fascinated and absolutely awestruck at what we find, and the harder you look and the more you know, you realize you don't know how cool every little new thing is, and it's just absolutely astounding to get into the stuff."[8]

Another biologist described the beauty and awe he experiences during observations of cells in his research:

> So it turns out that cells undergo this really intricate, delicate choreography in the sense that cells move in very precise directions, and they do it as groups, so it's kind of *the embryonic equivalent of line dancing*. . . . It is just utterly astonishing. Even though we're beginning to understand the molecules that control these cells as they do their dance, the dance itself is just perpetually amazing to me . . . and watching these glowing cells using these very sophisticated microscopes, I just never get tired of that.[9]

For some Christian scientists, their scientific work fills them with awe and wonder that strengthens not only their appreciation of science but also their deep sense of wonder of God. Throughout history, pursuit of God through the natural world has led a number of Christians to great scientific discoveries, and many Christian scientists today start their studies with the sense that they are pursuing God's beauty found in the natural world. For them, their scientific work is a form of worship that lets them better see and appreciate God's creation and brings them closer to God. "I think there are two things in science that you see. There's a lot of mystery and there's a lot of beauty," said a biologist I interviewed. "I think . . . mystery provokes wonder, and . . . beauty provokes awe." He went on, "This universe is inconceivably large and created, so I think there's this point where you just fall into worship when you see these things, and it's beautiful, so then it's amazing that [God] chose to make this world understandable to us too. I mean, in so many ways, it's really phenomenal. I mean, I encounter beauty every day."[10] A geneticist I spoke with echoed a similar sentiment: "It's this wonderful thrill of discovery not just on the natural plane but of a God who made that, you know?" he said. "And so it's really kind of cool and wonderfully awe-inspiring, and so it keeps me connected, right to God."[11]

Christian scientists also see beauty in the process of science and in the scientific career. They feel awed by the details uncovered and discoveries made. "A lot of what we spend time really learning, like how things work, . . . I'm really intrigued by. I think it's amazing how it works and who came up with it and how intricate everything is," one Christian physicist explained.[12] A Christian biologist, when asked if she saw beauty in her work, said, "I definitely see beauty and . . . even nonreligious scientists, that's why we do science. We're fascinated and absolutely awestruck at what we find, and the harder you look and the more you know, the more you realize you don't know and how cool every little new thing is, and it's just absolutely astounding."[13]

I quote all these Christian scientists talking about their scientific work itself—not only what they can do with the scientific work or the practical ways that it might help people (although these are certainly important)—so that you might see from scientists themselves how they find awe of God in the very nature of their scientific work. The act of doing scientific work itself is a way that they might worship God. And this experience of awe through scientific work is a way that they build common ground with scientists who are not Christians.

Awe in Nonreligious Scientists

My research has found that scientists who are nonreligious *also* experience feelings of awe and wonder at new discoveries, the beauty of the natural world, and the vastness and intricacies of what they examine and explore. One biologist told me, "I think my non-Christian colleagues, even my atheist colleagues, I really feel like they're on the doorstep of worship. Especially if they're good scientists, they are there [on the doorstep of worship] all the time."[14] This is his way of saying that he believes his nonreligious colleagues feel awe, reverence, and elation, which are traditionally thought of as emotions evoked by religious experiences.

A number of nonreligious scientists I have spoken with over my fifteen years of research have described experiencing beauty, awe, and wonder through their work. "I think that in particle astrophysics there's a lot of room for that because . . . you're dealing with the sort of very broad questions that span . . . billions of years of time and all of space and it's sort of easy to . . . kind of feel the bigness of it all," one nonreligious physicist said.[15] And a nonreligious biologist similarly told me, "I feel like on a daily basis, if I do experiments, I cherish the beauty of truths. For example, I stain some cells with pigments of what we call neon fluorescent . . . proteins. If we stain cells with some color, and you will see this spread . . . of the color, and it's like stars shining in the universe. . . . That's something I think is a privilege [of being a] scientist."[16]

A number of scientists spoke about feeling wonder at what has yet to be uncovered and observed and about feeling awe at how much more there is to discover. They also described the elation they feel when they do discover something new, an exhilaration that comes from solving a mystery and adding to our understanding of the world. One nonreligious scientist said, "I derive a great deal of satisfaction from understanding something after I've made a set of natural history observations or done experiments, like 'Oh, I know how that works now. I got it, this is how it happens, and I'm the only one in the world that knows that at least for this moment because I did it; I did the work, I asked the question and I answered it.' . . . So yeah I really—I love that part of it."[17] Another nonreligious scientist told me, "When you really understand things, that's another thing, that's another great pleasure. . . . There's a bunch of confusing effects and you really figure it out. You know that is just great. Now is it beauty or awe? . . . I certainly take a lot of pleasure in other people's results as well, when there's some new insight, some new cosmology measurement that tells you something that's new, that fits in as a piece of the puzzle, and that is pretty fantastic."[18]

Some nonreligious scientists even linked their sense of "scientific awe" to spirituality. One scientist, who does not consider himself to be part of any religious tradition, told me, "You know that feeling you get standing by the seashore looking out over the endless expanse of water—or standing in the rainforest listening to the insects and the birds and their huge diversity and incomprehensibility? Or the feeling you get considering the age of all things in existence and how long it could go on? Sort of awe at the totality of things? If that's what spirituality is, then I get it."[19] The sense of awe gained through pure scientific discovery is a type of antidote to the way we in Christian communities sometimes think of science. We think of it either in utilitarian terms, focusing on how we can use science through medical applications to help others (and this is good, but it is not the entire picture), or in terms of propositional statements, where we are noticing claims of science and filtering them to see how the claims of science compare to the claims of faith. Science is indeed these things. But here we are seeing that it is also much more. We are seeing that science is also an experience, a deep experience of awe over which the Christian scientist might build a bridge with scientists who do not have faith. And that deep experience of awe of God through science needs to be brought to church.

Bringing Scientific Awe to Church

In my research, I have found that Christians are "more likely to recommend that a child go into an applied science occupation, such as [being a] physician, than a pure science occupation, like [being a] biologist or a physicist."[20] Christians tend to view applied science roles as more clearly connected to some of the values and goals our faith emphasizes, such as helping others and reducing suffering. In one study I conducted, 24 percent of evangelicals and 27 percent of mainline Protestants said they considered themselves "very interested in new scientific discoveries."[21] Yet, when asked in the same survey if they agreed with the statement "scientific research is valuable even when it doesn't provide immediate tangible benefits," only 12 percent of evangelicals and 16 percent of mainline Protestants agreed—the lowest percentages of all religious groups surveyed.[22] In other words, Christians do not show the same level of support as other groups do for science done simply for the sake of scientific discovery. I believe this is partly because Christians are not aware of how—as I mentioned above—the practice of pure science can elicit awe, strengthen faith, and draw Christians closer to God.

This is where the testimonies of Christian and nonreligious scientists, like those we have heard in this chapter, can help. By sharing their personal experiences in science, Christian scientists can help other Christians experience "scientific awe." And in hearing nonreligious scientists express appreciation for the sacred qualities of scientific discovery, Christians may find something akin to faith. As a result, research suggests, Christians might be encouraged to pursue science themselves. A recent study found that those who are in awe of nature are more aware of the gaps in their knowledge and are thus more likely to explore scientific interests.[23]

How can we use science at church to experience awe of God? Church leaders can start by helping youth and their parents see science as a viable career path that will not hurt their faith but that actually has the potential to support and enrich it. For example, during a sermon, pastors could interview scientists about their experiences of appreciating beauty through science. Pastors could begin by preaching on Psalm 104, where the psalmist marvels at all that God has made and then include interviews with scientists. Or they could invite Christian scientists to talk about how their exploration of the natural world deepens their understanding of creation. Even better, they could organize events in which congregants directly experience the beauty of science for themselves—perhaps through hands-on experiments run by scientists or visits to a lab, observatory, or field site. In this way, congregants can experience firsthand the awe that science can evoke. The Christian writer Paul Tripp says, "God created an awesome world. God intentionally loaded the world with amazing things to leave you astounded. The carefully air-conditioned termite mound in Africa, the tart crunchiness of an apple, the explosion of thunder, the beauty of an orchid, the interdependent systems of the human body, the inexhaustible pounding of the ocean waves, and thousands of other created sights, sounds, touches, and tastes—God designed all to be awesome. And he intended you to be daily amazed."[24]

Further Discussion

1. When have you experienced feelings of awe? When have you felt awe outside of a church context?
2. What are your experiences with science? Have you ever felt a sense of awe because of nature or the natural world?
3. Do you see similarities between the awe felt by scientists and your own feelings of awe?

4. How can the language of awe help you better connect with and understand the work of scientists who are Christians?
5. How can the language of awe help you better connect with and understand the work of scientists who are not Christians?

10

Shalom

THE PRESSURES of being a researcher in the social sciences, which include applying for grants, teaching, mentoring, committee work, writing, and program management—alongside parenting, church work, and the ordinary inundations of modern living—make it hard for me to get to stillness. Here is one way I try: after I drop my daughter off at school in the morning, the first part of my prayer is my rendition of a phrase from Psalm 46:10 in the Hebrew Bible (the Christian Old Testament): "Be still, and know that I am God." I repeat the phrase "Let me be still and know that you are God" to myself as I walk to the university campus.

I walk quickly as I pray. "Let me be still . . ." Thoughts of what I need to get done in the work hours ahead and what I have left undone at home immediately assault me. "Let me be still . . ." As I get nearer to campus, I try to resist the urge to start listing the litany of things I need to do. "Let me be still . . ." As I wait for the light in front of campus to turn green, I stand on one foot and then the other, trying to get in a few balance exercises that my physical therapist told me to do every day after I had a joint in my toe replaced; I am easily distracted. "Let me be still . . ."

Once I am on campus and through the beautiful entrance with its ornate architecture, my walk takes me through a building-sized art installation, which has a square in the top that is open to the sky. When I remember, I stop there and look through the square. (Sky and clouds often make me feel closer to God.) It is here that I turn to the second part of my prayer: "Let me know that I am loved fully by God." I pray this piece of the prayer because I often feel there are so many people to impress as part of my work—colleagues, students, funders, and reviewers, to name just a few—and the culture of academic science is pressure-filled, highly competitive, and at times cutthroat. I often feel too limited. "Let me know that I am fully loved," that I have been created with everything I need in order to do what I need to do.

The last part of my walk takes me up several flights of stairs. With each step, I repeat the third part of my prayer: "Let me enter into what you are doing today." When I arrive at my office at the earliest times, before the sun fully rises, I am excited to be there. I take joy in my work and see it as having a higher purpose. On the not so good days, I hustle into my office and the work ahead of me; I often consider skipping the walk to get to work faster in the car. But on the better days, I remind myself that I am participating in what God is doing in the world.

I do not solely work for myself, and my duty is beyond the self. I work for the academics I collaborate with and those who read my work. I work for the students I mentor and teach. I work for the public outside the university, for whom I try to explain my research in a way that helps them better understand the world and themselves. I work for my funders, who have their own goals and missions. I work from the place of community-based virtues like equality and justice. I feel a responsibility to use my scientific work to accomplish something meaningful, improve social problems, and help people flourish.

In my interviews with Christian scientists, I have found that many of them feel similarly about their work and their goals, sometimes drawing on the concepts of shalom and stewardship. *Shalom* is a Hebrew word that comes from a root that means "completeness" and "perfection," and it refers to the peace, harmony, well-being, and prosperity that result from the flourishing of all creation.[1] *Shalom* can mean to get involved in the messiness of the world, to try to change structures that are not just, to try to make them more just. Stewardship, or caring for the world (especially in the form of environmental protection), is often thought of as a scientific virtue, but it is a deeply Christian virtue as well, a practice that brings us closer to shalom. Christian stewardship encompasses the idea of unique humanness, that we were created by God and thus have a responsibility to care for and look after the rest of God's creation.

As a sociologist, the twin virtues of shalom and stewardship and their related virtue of justice are ones that I have pondered a lot. They seem to be the ones best cultivated in my own discipline, which is deeply concerned with helping the other, not only on an individual basis but also in a way that may change whole structures of societies, like governments, social services, or even churches, so that they might better operate toward shalom. Theologian Walter Brueggemann writes in *The Prophetic Imagination*, "Jesus in his solidarity with the marginal ones is moved to compassion. Compassion constitutes a radical form of criticism for it announces that the hurt is to be taken seriously, that the hurt is not to be accepted as normal and natural but is an abnormal and unacceptable condition for humanness. . . . Thus the compassion of Jesus is not to be understood as a personal emotional reaction but as a public criticism in which he dares to act upon his concern against the entire numbness of the social context."[2]

Christians are not original in our focus on stewardship. Christian stewardship is similar to the Jewish concept of *tikkun olam*, which I heard about from members of different Jewish traditions when I asked about their understanding of science.[3] "I think that it is absolutely fundamental to the Jewish faith to take care of the earth, to respect it, to not be wasteful, to be appreciative of the bounty, and to try to take care of it as much as possible," a Jewish law professor told me during one of my studies. He continued, "You know, we believe very much in . . . issues of justice, and we have a belief called *tikkun olam,* which means heal the world."[4] Translated literally, *tikkun olam* means "world repair," and it has evolved from a minor doctrine into a driving force for modern Jewish social justice and policy reform. For those of Jewish faith, working to make the world better and more harmonious is both a tenet of their religion and an important aspect of their daily lives. The hope is to bring about shalom.

When I interviewed religious scientists in India, they did not use the terms *stewardship*, *shalom*, or *tikkun olam*, but they explained the driving force behind their scientific work using similar concepts. One biologist, for example, spoke about feeling compelled to use his work for the benefit of others. "If you walk out of campus . . . you will see a bunch of kids with no clothes on their backs," he said. "So you think immediately, I just spent a million dollars on [scientific technology for my experiments]. . . . I better get something out of it that hopefully is useful for somebody in the future."[5]

For many religious scientists in India, being a "good scientist" means doing work that alleviates suffering and poverty. This was a theme that came up often in my interviews. "Our [science] institute is the temple. So all the time we pray here in our own lab so that God can bless us. Physically, we do not pray, but working here is like praying to God," said one physics professor. "So we are always trying to find something new . . . that will be useful for our society."[6]

My studies have found that many Christians in science also see their scientific work as a way to help create a more just and peaceful world, and they allow virtues and principles of their faith to affect how they use their science in the world.[7] "Christian scientists are motivated to be justice-bringers," one Christian biologist told me, explaining that "it's kind of a feeling sometimes like we are the sirens, maybe more so than in some other fields and as much as that may make you feel like you have an important job in the world."[8]

"He Has Made Me for Science"

One of my favorite movies of all time is the 1981 British film *Chariots of Fire*. There is one line in particular that many of us who have seen the movie remember. Eric Liddell's sister is reprimanding him for neglecting his responsibilities before God as a missionary as he devotes his focus to competitive running. Liddell responds, "I believe that God made me for a purpose. But He also made me fast, and when I run, I feel His pleasure."[9] Many of the Christian scientists I have surveyed and interviewed over the years view their scientific work as a calling and a way that they feel God's pleasure and live out God's purpose for them. This purpose is often seen as fulfilling their responsibilities as God's stewards. Many also believe that viewing their scientific work through the lens of their Christian faith helps them see ways they can use their work toward shalom.

I have met Christian scientists who have selected certain research areas or projects because they believe they will benefit society, create positive relationships with colleagues, or foster virtues like patience, kindness, and humility in the scientific community and in the broader society. I have spoken with Christian scientists who have specifically chosen work that will help alleviate poverty or suffering or who have declined funding from a source that might use their research to contribute to nuclear proliferation or to harm the environment. Other Christian scientists draw on their faith and their sense of purpose to help them deal with the demands and competition that define a career in science, to help them keep going in the face of personal or family challenges, to infuse meaning into mundane work, or to instill that same purpose in their students. Some describe being divinely called to practice science.

"I see all of the different parts of the scientific career as a calling, with the idea that vocation is God's calling for your life," said Jaime, a Christian evolutionary biologist we met earlier. "Our standards—as Christians—of scholarship are always intertwined with our standards for teaching and engaging students to uncover their own calling as well as to train them to be excellent scientists."[10]

"I definitely pray regularly. And I pray that the outcomes of my work would be meaningful and helpful to people," said a Christian immunologist who works on very rare disorders that attack the disease-fighting systems in children's bodies. "You know, I always ask for God's best in my work. But . . . if I'm just focused on my own kind of academic achievements and outputs it might *not* be." His prayer, he said, is that he would see science as a kind of mission field that allows him to live out a higher purpose. He told me, "I see science as an amazing *tool* to intervene on the human condition . . . where there is suffering, where there are children who did not choose to have this immune deficiency and be in and out of the hospital. You know, we seek to understand and learn more about the science and biology, and drive at the root of the biology. [We want to] tweak the biology or transplant, so that child can have a meaningful, healthy life. And I look at that as a calling and a mission."[11]

One evangelical Christian biologist told me that he sees his work as "really much more of an integrated calling." Echoing *Chariots of Fire*, he said, "God made me for this. To be a full

Christian is to be fully what he has made me for, and he has made me for science."[12]

Stewarding the Environment

One survey I conducted found that 28 percent of evangelicals and 31 percent of mainline Protestants say they are "very interested" in caring for the environment.[13] But climate and environmental scientists have also told me they sometimes meet Christians who are hesitant to discuss caring for the environment as a piece of Christian stewardship, as a piece of bringing God's shalom to the world. Some Christians are quite vocal against environmental efforts, worrying that placing so much emphasis on caring for the environment will lead us to neglect caring for humans. I have experienced these attitudes firsthand in my studies. One church youth minister, for example, explained to me his view: "If we have the opportunity, we should help take care of this planet that we've been given. Having said that, I also believe that the value of human life is higher than the value of a whale or a species of monkey."[14]

Many Christian scientists, however, see environmental care, or climate change research, as tied to caring for people and as one way we fulfill our responsibility as stewards of the earth. For these Christians, repairing and caring for the environment and addressing climate change is a way to show appreciation, respect, and reverence for God and for all of God's creation. "For Christians, doing something about climate change is about living our faith—caring for those who need our help, our neighbors here at home or on the other side of the world, and taking responsibility for this planet that God created and entrusted to us," says Katharine Hayhoe, a scientist and evangelical Christian who is vocal about the intersection of stewardship and caring for the climate.[15]

The National Association of Evangelicals, which represents more than 45,000 local churches from forty different denominations, has explained its motivation to care for the environment this way: "To provide scientific expertise toward specific altruistic goals, to offer excellent medical practices on behalf of the sick, to produce healthy food for those who are hungry, to offer assistance in the preservation of the environment and to strive for the stewardship of natural resources—all of these things demonstrate a high calling, extending common grace around the globe."[16]

One evangelical biology professor told me, "We're talking here about the biblical basis for environmental stewardship . . . the responsibility that we have to take care of the world around us." He continued, "I remember a theologian a few years ago that said the pollution of [our] lake was blasphemous. In other words, . . . God made all this and then what we were doing was just like taking a beautiful painting and throwing paint at it or something."[17] It reminded me of the words in Jeremiah 2:7:

> I brought you into a fertile land
> to enjoy its fruits and rich produce.
> But you came and defiled my land
> and made my inheritance detestable.

A Christian physicist I interviewed told me,

> I always kind of start from the basis of human beings as being created in the image of God with the specific purpose of being the stewards of God's creation and, in light of that, we understand that the world is good and it's beautiful and it's understandable and acceptable to us. And we should try to understand it as best as we can and that we should not just try to understand it but also preserve it and protect it. I think this is our job. So that would affect the way that I look at environmental policy.[18]

A Christian physician I spoke with said, "Throughout the world, the poor are often victims of environmental degradation. And so one of the most important things that the Bible teaches us is that what God most cares about is the poor. . . . And so to the extent that degradation of the environment is harming the poor and making them even worse off, then it is an essential issue for Christians to get engaged in."[19]

In one study I conducted, I met a pastor who told me he sees "science as a tool from God that humans can use to help each other and improve the quality of life." His congregation, he said, cares for the environment by recycling, buying natural products, and hosting events aimed at exploring the relationship between faith and creation. "In the book of Genesis . . . God gave the garden to humankind. . . . Some theologians think that the garden is the representation of the entire earth. God gave earth to humankind to care for. . . . We're supposed to take care of the earth," he said. "What does that include? It includes animals. It includes air. . . . Let me say this: We receive a great deal of inspiration from Scripture about how to be good stewards. We want to be good stewards."[20]

Other churches should follow this lead, introducing environmental care to their congregants through practice as well as preaching. Environmental care is not often a topic addressed in churches, which could be part of the reason some Christians do not feel comfortable discussing environmental issues or climate change. Even small-scale actions, such as cleaning up a local area or working to reduce waste in the church or community, can help Christians see environmental care as a way of caring for people.

Wholeness through Diversity

Several Christian scientists I interviewed explicitly discussed increasing representation and equality in science as one of their goals and one of the ways they enter into shalom through their work as scientists. Some of these scientists specifically connect their faith to their efforts to increase opportunities for those who are underrepresented in science. Studying and increasing diversity in science is an area about which I am particularly passionate as a sociologist who is a Christian. Some of those I have interviewed for my studies join me in this. Jaime, the evolutionary biologist, for example, spoke about being on the committee within her guild that works to promote and represent diversity in her scientific field and about how fighting for diversity in science can be very much a piece of one's faith: "I find that the other people who are on that committee also tend to be people who have some sort of faith tradition—whether or not they talk about it a lot, they see their way of living out their faith as working very hard to increase opportunities for people who . . . otherwise wouldn't have opportunities in science."[21]

When we look at the US scientific community, we see that nonwhites, especially African Americans and Latinos/as, are vastly underrepresented in science. For example, black Americans, who comprise 12 to 14 percent of the US population, make up just over 1 percent of all those who have careers in science, medicine, or technology. Women of all ethnic and racial groups are also underrepresented in the basic sciences and some forms of medicine. While women represent more than 50 percent of the overall US population, they represent less than 10 percent of many science fields. Yet, African Americans, Latinos/as, and white women are all overrepresented in churches. Nearly 80 percent of black Americans see themselves as committed Christians, and nearly 77 percent of Latinos/as see themselves as Catholics, Protestants, or evangelical Christians.[22] One reason African Americans and Latinos/as are underrepresented in science is that they are more likely to attend lower-resourced schools with poorer science education. A related problem is that Christians of color don't often hear about scientists who believe like them or see scientists who look like them. One Christian geneticist I met, one of the few black women in her field at an elite university, was the first woman and the first African American to become head of a genetics program. During the five years she spent as a student, she said, there was only one black speaker brought in for her department's weekly seminar.[23] For many African Americans, science is "a no-trespassing zone," one black pastor said.[24] A Latino pastor told me, "I do think . . . it is helpful to have somebody of your own skin color [in science], because . . . to see one of your own would give an inspiration."[25]

Representation matters, and the lack of representation of women, people of color, and Christians in science is an issue that ought to concern the church. If Christians don't see themselves in the scientific enterprise, it becomes unlikely that they will follow that career path—and with fewer Christians in science, it becomes more difficult to show that science can be compatible with our faith.

Those who have been and are most marginalized in our society often are deeply compelled to fight against structures that marginalize others. One of the best ways to encourage Christians to enter science might be to frame science as a calling that provides an avenue for stewardship. Science can offer Christians many different opportunities to work toward repairing, healing, and protecting God's creation. The science career can be used not only to care for the environment but also to care for people in the interest of justice, equality, and human flourishing. Christians should understand how a scientific career can allow them to contribute to shalom. Church leaders can help by inviting scientists to talk with congregants about how they use their scientific work to bring positive change to the world. "Every four years or so, we do have a science and Christian faith kind of all-day seminar, and . . . we try to have some scientists come and talk about how amazing the natural world is, and just to kind of get students marinating in the joy of discovery," one scientist shared. He continued, "We need to do a lot better job of that [on a week-to-week basis], like providing opportunities

. . . during worship services [for people in churches to talk about their scientific work]. . . . I think we could do a better job in our youth curriculum. We don't really do much right now in the sciences, and I think having students hang out with scientists who are faithful followers of Christ and just allowing those students to pick the brains of these scientists could be really good."[26]

Churches also need to ensure that underrepresented students of color have access to science resources and that voices long ignored are included in their dialogues on science and faith. "If you look at the faith-science conversation in particular, it's mainly white people," an evangelical biologist said. He argued, "We need to engage the *entire* church in the United States on faith and science issues. [How we engage on faith and science] really does include black churches and Latino/a churches and Asian churches too. And their experience is different and so they might have different questions and so we should at least ask them, and I think it's really striking that there may be resistance to that."[27]

This evangelical biologist also told me that his focus on the virtues underlying stewardship and shalom have helped him connect with nonreligious colleagues and earn their respect and support. They stand on common ground in what they hope their work will accomplish. "They can see that I'm working to really serve the common good, to build bridges, and to work for peace," he said, "and *that* counts for so much for them, even if they disagree on particulars."[28]

Further Discussion

1. What do *shalom* and *stewardship* mean to you? How can you practice these concepts in your community or through your work?

2. Where are you most passionate about seeing more equality or justice brought to the world?
3. How might science be used as a tool to bring equality or justice in the areas in which you are passionate?
4. How can your congregation help its members cultivate shalom in the world?
5. How can your church and you as an individual engage in creating different structures and cultures, ones that better contribute to human flourishing?

11

Gratitude

I AM ALWAYS SUSPICIOUS of three-step techniques that promise to change my life, so when my pastor paused at the beginning of the service one day and asked members of the congregation to write down three things from the previous week they were grateful for, I thought it was a bit hokey. But over time, my cynicism waned and this practice has worked its way into my life. In fact, it has become so meaningful that I now have trouble starting the day without writing down several things for which I am thankful to God.

I am thankful for my family, and for my work and the meaning it brings to my life. I am thankful for my faith community and for my personal knowledge and experience of faith, which has given my life a deeper sense of meaning and purpose. I am also grateful for science and medicine, which have prolonged my life and improved its quality. I am particularly grateful for Yellapragada Subbarow, an Indian biochemist who developed a drug called methotrexate. Though this drug was originally meant to treat cancer, it revolutionized how I felt during a flare up of my disease in my early twenties, about ten years after my diagnosis. The flare up was crippling. I had so much pain in my arms that I could not lift a brush to my hair. I felt helpless, and I wasn't sure what my future would hold. Though Subbarow subscribed to a form of Hinduism, I can relate to his belief that "science merely prolongs life—religion deepens it"[1]—words that were inscribed on a plaque in his honor, located near the entrance of an antibiotic manufacturing facility in Bombay. I am grateful that God brought Subbarow and the rheumatologist who thought to prescribe methotrexate to me into my life. I am also grateful for advances in science and medicine that have reduced suffering, brought healing, and generally improved the lives of others. Indeed, I am in agreement with the 85 percent of Christians I have surveyed who think that science and medicine bring good to the world.[2]

The Parent of All Virtues

Gifts like these lead to gratitude. The psalmist writes,

> Great is the Lord and most worthy of praise;
> his greatness no one can fathom. (Ps. 145:3)

Gratitude is a core tenet of the Christian faith. Expressing gratitude is a way of showing our appreciation for the gifts bestowed on us by God and by others. Gratitude is also a way of remembering and acknowledging the good in our lives. "Gratitude is the truest approach to life," writes Robert Emmons, a psychologist at the University of California, Davis, and a contributor to Biola University's Center for Christian Thought. "We did not create or fashion ourselves. We did not birth ourselves. Life is about giving, receiving, and repaying. We are receptive beings, dependent on the help of others, on their gifts and their kindness."[3] Gratitude is a common theme throughout the Bible.

King David, the second king of Israel and the slayer of Goliath, is said to have prayed in 1 Chronicles 29:12–14: "Wealth and honor come from [God]. . . . We give you thanks, and praise your glorious name. . . . Everything comes from you."[4] Psalm 136:1 reads,

> Give thanks to the Lord, for he is good.
> His love endures forever.

Greek philosopher Cicero called gratitude "not only the greatest, but also the parent of all other virtues."[5] Deep gratitude reminds me of the concept of common grace, the idea that all good things come from God, whether or not they occur in a specifically Christian environment.

Science also reveals that gratitude is good for us. A number of scientific studies have shown that gratitude has significant physical and psychological benefits. It makes our hearts healthier, our minds stronger, and increases our sense of well-being. For example, one study of patients with heart failure found that higher levels of gratitude led to better sleep, less fatigue, and lower levels of inflammation.[6] Expressing gratitude has this effect because it activates the calming part of our nervous system, which can decrease cortisol (stress) levels and maybe even increase oxytocin (the bonding hormone babies trigger in mothers), a chemical that makes us feel good.[7] Gratitude may also be linked to a decreased desire to accrue more possessions and to a lower likelihood of burnout in the workplace.[8] A study of university students found that those who practiced gratitude in the form of thanking others, thanking God, cherishing blessings, appreciating hardships, and cherishing the moment had greater life satisfaction and felt positive feelings more often.[9] Studies also suggest that people who are more grateful may experience lower levels of depression and be more resilient after experiencing a traumatic event.[10]

I believe focusing on the virtue of gratitude could help Christians better connect and communicate with scientists. Through my studies and my personal experiences, I have found that the experience of gratitude is antithetical to anger and fear, emotions many Christians feel toward some scientific findings and scientists.[11] "What was so unique in the African-American church [that I work in] . . . is that it is a theology rooted in gratitude, rather than suspicion, which is a very different posture for addressing whatever life issues come your way. And it separates how you would approach science [or a scientist] or how you would approach theological questions, whether God is good; you know [the theology] already accepted that God is good," one Christian leader told me. "You may not understand how it works, but you're OK with not being able to understand."[12] According to the writer Diana Butler Bass, who has recently written a book on gratitude, "Gratitude is the emotional response to the surprise of our very existence, to sensing that inner light and realizing the astonishing sacred, social, and scientific events that brought each one of us into being."[13] We then can cry out like the psalmist, "I am fearfully and wonderfully made!" (Ps. 139:14).

Gratitude in Science

In my studies, several Christian scientists have expressed gratitude toward science. They feel grateful for science's abilities to reduce suffering and better the world. They also feel a tremendous sense of gratitude, *often gratitude to God*, that they can be a part of this endeavor and change. As one scientist put it, "We have science to help us understand how is it that this body with all of this complexity gets formed, and we have the science that is trying to deal with questions of evolution, for example. And then the whole space science and astronomy just totally declares the glory of God in the heavens."[14]

And science allows these scientists to feel that they are having a positive impact on God's creation and that they are a part of something larger than themselves. They also often describe science as a mission or calling that allows them to fulfill their purpose while pursuing their passion in a line of work they truly love. "The verse that 'to whom much is given much is expected' [comes] to mind—and, you know, that's one that's come to mind many a time," one Christian who works in biomedicine said about his scientific work. "You know, there's a debt to repay and I see science as an amazing *tool* to intervene on the human condition."[15] My studies have also found that while nonreligious scientists do not connect their work to a higher power or express gratitude toward God, they do give thanks for the beauty of the world and the processes they study, and many are thankful for their ability to affect change through their scientific work. Nonreligious scientists also expressed feeling profoundly grateful for the people who work alongside them: the coworkers and friends who support and help them in their endeavors. It reminded me of the feelings Christians have for the members of their churches and faith communities.

Christian scientists are often especially grateful for colleagues who understand that scientists can be religious, believe people of faith have a place in the scientific community, and are open to sincere and civil dialogue about the relationship between science and religion. For example, Jaime explained how grateful she was for her non-Christian colleagues:

> I've never received any hostility for being a Christian through graduate school—whereas a lot of my students, who are in graduate school, definitely keep [their faith] on the down low and say that there are open comments that the senior faculty will make, comments both to undergraduates as well as to graduate students that "Christians are stupid." . . . I understand that those types of comments and that attitude definitely exist . . .

> but I have not personally experienced it. . . . I've been *extremely* fortunate in my life experiences, because I know that it is not, it is just not always the case. . . . I have had opportunities for *real* dialogue and real questions that I am super grateful for.[16]

Christians Are Grateful for Science and Scientists

It may be surprising, but many of the Christians (those who are not themselves scientists) I interviewed for my research expressed deep gratitude for science. They are grateful for the ways in which science makes the world a better place. Some described being grateful for science in general and the role it plays in their lives, while others focused on particular medical advances. "There are levels of science that are very helpful and very important to the growth of our society and the development of our society," said one man who attends what he called an African American Baptist church. "Not only do I not have polio because of the grace of God," he said, "but [also] because I took the vaccine when I was a child." He is also thankful for the scientists who work in medicine. "You see people praying for healing and believing in healing," he said, "and thanking God when the doctor does a good surgery."[17] Another Christian expressed gratitude to scientists for the research they do on Alzheimer's, a disease her mother had.[18]

"I am an enormous fan of science," one evangelical Christian man told me during an interview. "I find it fascinating. I find the people who dedicate their lives to [science, they are] servants of humanity. And what they do excites me as amongst some of the most important things that happen in human civilization." He continued, expressing his gratitude for all the future opportunities science can create: "I would love to see us propel science forward . . . at the speed—the maximum speed possible to have helpful outcomes. And I think we should do everything we can to encourage it . . . and use everything available to us and revealed to us to the advantage of the species."[19] In one survey I conducted, I found that about 71 percent of evangelicals and 72 percent of mainline Protestants agreed that "because of science and technology, there will be more opportunities for the next generation."[20]

A number of Christian scientists even described feeling gratitude for the ways that science complements their faith. "I am very thankful for all of these medical scientists who came up with [these developments in medicine], and God gave them the brain power to figure it out and created the universe in a way that made it possible," an evangelical Christian shared.[21] "Science . . . has made me really appreciate the complexity and beauty in life," another Christian told me. "And to me that makes me more spiritual, if anything."[22]

Christian Scientists Are Grateful for Faith

Christians in science that I have interviewed also talked about feeling grateful for their faith and the impact it can have on their work. One Christian physicist I interviewed said that faith had called him to science, providing both motivation and support for his scientific work. As a scientist, "faith is very much part and parcel of, at least for me, what I do," he explained, "and [faith] makes it a rational thing to do." He recalled mentoring a Christian student who wrote as his dissertation dedication, "Hallelujah! All glory and praise be to God! As I reflect on my quarter-century of formal education, I cannot help but marvel at the innumerable blessings God has bestowed upon me. Let this dissertation be my prayer of thanksgiving to God, who has granted me the ability to study His Creation these past years. It has been among the most enjoyable pursuits of my life." After our interview, the physicist sent me an email expanding on this recollection. He told me the student "might have written this regardless of who his adviser was, but I'd like to think that at least I made him comfortable to do so."[23] He felt grateful that his faith allowed him to connect with his student in this way and to encourage the student to express his faith freely.

Christians in medicine-related fields described feeling grateful for the comfort faith can bring for those who are suffering. When I asked a Christian biologist if he had ever been in a situation where he felt his faith mattered, he told me, "I remember several times where I would encounter a patient who was having a particularly difficult situation—either they were, you know, end-stage lung cancer or some kind of disease that clearly there was no cure [for]. . . . Praying with them and sharing a sincere compassion hopefully that they felt around that . . . I've had experiences like that for sure."[24]

It might surprise you to hear that, under certain conditions, scientists who are *not* religious appreciate religion. Some feel it can add depth to an understanding of the world and the meaning of life. The late paleontologist and agnostic Stephen Jay Gould, for example, believed that science and religion govern separate parts of the world and our lives (he calls them "non-overlapping magisteria") and that both are essential. "The lack of conflict between science and religion arises from the lack of overlap between their respective domains of professional expertise—science in the empirical constitution of the universe, and religion in the search for proper ethical values and spiritual meaning of our lives," he writes. "The attainment of wisdom in a full life requires extensive attention to both domains—for a great book tells us that the truth can make us free and that we will live in optimal harmony with our fellows when we learn to do justly, love mercy, and walk humbly."[25]

A number of years ago, I conducted a survey on what US scientists think about religion, and I spoke with a number of atheist and agnostic scientists. Of the 275 atheist scientists I interviewed face to face, only five were "so hostile that they were actively working against religion."[26] Some of the atheist and agnostic scientists attended or were involved in churches, and some saw church as a place where they could teach their children about morality and community. I have been surprised to learn through my studies that "religion also provides some scientists with important ethical guidelines," and they believe that talking about this openly will "help the general religious public understand how some scientists utilize religion in thinking about the implications of their work."[27] One physicist who does not believe in God told me he sees positive aspects of religion, such as "social structures for people, engagement, belonging." He also believes that, depending on the church, religion can "be a good intellectual self-evaluation, self-fulfilling experience."[28] An atheist biologist said the "social aspects of religion" were "very important."[29] I have also met nonreligious scientists who are "spiritual atheists," meaning that even though they are not religious, they feel spirituality can help them understand "key mysteries about the world."[30]

Finding Common Ground

Nearly twenty years ago, I told my grandfather, a farmer, that I was going to get a PhD in sociology and that it would probably take four years or more (it took six!). He asked, "After you get the PhD, will you make more money than you would without one?" I told him I wasn't sure, but I wasn't doing it for the money. "If you aren't doing it for the money," he asked, "then why are you devoting your life to that?" The question stopped me in my tracks. At the time, I wasn't really sure how to answer. While my grandfather's question did not stop me from getting a PhD, it did have an impact on my life in another way, perhaps even more profound. It has become an orienting principle of my life, a call to pause and make sure that I am devoting my time and effort to something of value and virtue.

It is no accident that I end this book on the topic of gratitude. Some scientists now believe that gratitude is an inherent part of our human nature, a virtue and emotion with deep roots.[31] It helps us give and receive, build better relationships, and engender reciprocity. It leads to alliances that benefit our survival. Gratitude extends our thinking beyond ourselves and leads to collaborations that can beget a greater sense of community. Gratitude helps us stop and reflect, improves our patience and self-control. Perhaps, then, gratitude can be a first step in helping each of us and our church communities improve the relationship between science and our faith—reminding us to be thankful for the benefits that each provides, the value each brings to our lives, and the ways in which they can work together.

Now, looking back, I have an answer to my grandfather's question: I am devoting my life to sociology, and to the sociological study of religion, because of *gratitude*. I am grateful for my Christian faith and the role it plays in my life. I am grateful for my church community. I am also grateful for the advances that science and social science have made in helping us better understand and navigate our world. I am grateful for the scientific tools and concepts that allow us to better get along and work together. Indeed, my gratitude for both faith and science has compelled me to study faith communities and scientific communities and to endeavor to give back to both of those communities. *And because of this gratitude I can say that my work is part of my worship.*

Further Discussion

1. What are you grateful for in life? How do you see gratitude affecting your life?

2. What are some practical ways that you can practice gratitude daily? Write down two of them.
3. Take a moment to write down three things you are grateful for about science. Share these things.
4. Could you write a note to someone you know who works in a scientific field to express gratitude for them and their work?

Further Reading

Chapter 1

Elaine Howard Ecklund and Christopher P. Scheitle, *Religion vs. Science: What Religious People Really Think* (New York: Oxford University Press, 2017).

Scott MacDonald and Eleonore Stump, eds., *Aquinas's Moral Theory: Essays in Honor of Norman Kretzmann* (Ithaca, NY: Cornell University Press, 2008).

Alasdair MacIntyre, *After Virtue: A Study in Moral Theory*, 3rd ed. (Notre Dame, IN: University of Notre Dame Press, 2007).

Christopher Pieper, *Sociology as a Spiritual Practice: How Studying Sociology Can Make You a Better Person* (Dubuque, IA: Kendall Hunt, 2015).

Chapter 2

Dietrich Bonhoeffer, *Life Together: The Classic Exploration of Christian Community* (San Francisco: HarperOne, 2009). This is my favorite book on Christian community.

Elaine Howard Ecklund, *Science vs. Religion: What Scientists Really Think* (New York: Oxford University Press, 2010). This is my own book on the US science community.

Joseph C. Hermanowicz, *The Stars Are Not Enough: Scientists—Their Passions and Professions* (Chicago: University of Chicago Press, 1998). This book gives more information on the science community.

Tom McLeish, *The Poetry and Music of Science: Comparing Creativity in Science and Art* (Oxford: Oxford University Press, 2019).

Chapter 3

Denis Alexander, *Creation or Evolution—Do We Have to Choose?* (n.p.: Monarch, 2014).

Francis Collins, *The Language of God: A Scientist Presents Evidence for Belief* (New York: Free Press, 2007).

John H. Evans, *What Is a Human? What the Answers Mean for Human Rights* (New York: Oxford University Press, 2016).

Deborah B. Haarsma and Loren D. Haarsma, *Origins: Christian Perspectives on Creation, Evolution, and Intelligent Design* (Grand Rapids: Faith Alive Christian Resources, 2011).

Ronald Numbers, *The Creationists: From Scientific Creationism to Intelligent Design* (Cambridge, MA: Harvard University Press, 2006).

Chapter 4

Elias Baumgarten, "Curiosity as a Moral Virtue," *The International Journal of Applied Philosophy* 15, no. 2 (2001): 169–84. This article is an excellent resource for the philosophically curious.

Greg Cootsona, *Mere Science and Christian Faith: Bridging the Divide with Emerging Adults* (Downers Grove, IL: InterVarsity, 2018).

Mario Livio, *Why? What Makes Us Curious* (New York: Simon & Schuster, 2017).

Chapter 5

Peter Berger and Anton Zijderveld, *In Praise of Doubt: How to Have Convictions without Becoming a Fanatic* (New York: HarperOne, 2009).

Anne Lamott, *Plan B: Further Thoughts on Faith* (New York: Riverhead Books, 2006).

Vance Morgan, "Why Doubt Is My Favorite Virtue," Patheos, *Freelance Christianity* (blog), April 27, 2019, https://www.patheos.com/blogs/freelancechristianity/why-doubt-is-my-favorite-virtue.

Henri J. M. Nouwen, *The Inner Voice of Love: A Journey through Anguish to Freedom* (Cincinnati: St. Anthony Messenger Press, 2001).

John Ortberg, *Know Doubt: The Importance of Embracing Uncertainty in Your Faith* (Grand Rapids: Zondervan, 2008).

Chapter 6

Ian M. Church and Peter L. Samuelson, *Intellectual Humility: An Introduction to the Philosophy and Science* (New York: Bloomsbury Academic, 2017).

Karl E. Johnson and Keith Yoder, "Chemist as Complementarian: An Interview with Robert C. Fay," *Perspectives on Science and Christian Faith* 61, no. 4 (2009): 233–39.

Everett L. Worthington Jr. and Scott T. Allison, *Heroic Humility: What the Science of Humility Can Say to People Raised on Self-Focus* (Washington, DC: American Psychological Association, 2018).

Chapter 7

John H. Evans, *Contested Reproduction: Genetic Technologies, Religion, and Public Debate* (Chicago: University of Chicago Press, 2010). This is the best academic work on the religious and ethical issues related to reproductive genetic technologies.

Dorothy Sayers, *The Mind of the Maker* (New York: HarperSanFrancisco, 1941). This is a wonderful book on creativity.

Chapter 8

Kate Bowler, *Everything Happens for a Reason: And Other Lies I've Loved* (New York: Random House, 2018). This is the best book on suffering I have read.

John H. Evans, *Playing God? Human Genetic Engineering and the Rationalization of Public Bioethical Debate* (Chicago: University of Chicago Press, 2002).

John H. Evans, "The Road to Enhancement, via Human Gene Editing, Is Paved with Good Intentions," *The Conversation*, November 27, 2018, http://theconversation.com/the-road-to-enhancement-via-human-gene-editing-is-paved-with-good-intentions-107677.

Chapter 9

Robert Gilbert, *Science and the Truthfulness of Beauty: How the Personal Perspective Discovers Creation* (Abingdon, UK: Routledge, 2018). Gilbert is a professor of biophysics and an Anglican priest at Oxford; this is a book for those interested in discovering beauty through science.

Paul David Tripp, *Awe: Why It Matters for Everything We Think, Say, and Do* (Wheaton: Crossway, 2015). This book is not specifically about science but about the importance of awe in the Christian life.

Chapter 10

Walter Brueggemann, *The Prophetic Imagination*, 2nd ed. (Minneapolis: Fortress, 2001). This is not a book about science but a book about power and change throughout the Bible.

Andy Crouch, *Culture Making: Recovering Our Creative Calling* (Downers Grove, IL: InterVarsity, 2008). Crouch deals with what it means for Christians to get involved in the messiness of creating culture.

Elaine Howard Ecklund and Anne E. Lincoln, *Failing Families, Failing Science: Work-Family Conflict in Academic Science* (New York: New York University Press, 2016). This book deals with gender and family life in science, which are issues that prevent many from succeeding in science, particularly Christian women.

Katharine Hayhoe and Andrew Farley, *A Climate for Change: Global Warming Facts for Faith-Based Decisions* (New York: Faith Words, 2009). Hayhoe, who was one of *Time* magazine's one hundred most influential people of 2014, is a sought-after speaker on the issue of climate change and faith.

"Science Benefits from Diversity," editorial, *Nature* 558, no. 5 (June 2018), https://www.nature.com/articles/d41586-018-05326-3.

Chapter 11

Andrea Brandt, "Science Proves That Gratitude Is Key to Well Being," July 30, 2018, *Psychology Today*, https://www.psychologytoday.com/us/blog/mindful-anger/201807/science-proves-gratitude-is-key-well-being.

Diana Butler Bass, *Grateful: The Transformative Power of Giving Thanks* (San Francisco: HarperOne, 2018). This is my favorite book on gratitude.

Anne Lamott, *Help, Thanks, Wow: The Three Essential Prayers* (New York: Riverhead Books, 2012). I love Lamott's grittiness, and I learned a good deal about gratitude from this book.

Notes

Chapter 1 From Fear to Understanding

1. A thorough exploration of virtues is beyond the scope of this work, but for those interested, see St. Thomas Aquinas, *Treatise on the Virtues*, trans. John A. Oesterle (Notre Dame, IN: University of Notre Dame Press, 1992).

As an undergraduate at Cornell University in the mid-1990s, I took a class with Norman Kretzmann on Aquinas that changed my life. Kretzmann's former colleagues and students have put together a volume that discusses Aquinas's moral ideas. See Scott MacDonald and Eleonore Stump, eds., *Aquinas's Moral Theory: Essays in Honor of Norman Kretzmann* (Ithaca, NY: Cornell University Press, 2008).

2. There is a lot of writing on sociology of organizations and organizational cultures. If you are interested in this literature, one initial book I would suggest is Joanne Martin, *Cultures in Organizations: Three Perspectives* (New York: Oxford University Press, 1992).

3. My first book on what US natural and social scientists think about religion is *Science vs. Religion: What Scientists Really Think* (New York: Oxford University Press, 2010).

4. Much of this research background is discussed in my most recent academic book, Elaine Howard Ecklund and Christopher P. Scheitle, *Religion vs. Science: What Religious People Really Think* (New York: Oxford University Press, 2017).

5. See Nancy T. Ammerman, *Bible Believers: Fundamentalists in the Modern World* (New Brunswick, NJ: Rutgers University Press, 1987); George M. Marsden, *Understanding Fundamentalism and Evangelicalism* (Grand Rapids: Eerdmans, 1991); Christian Smith, *American Evangelicalism: Embattled and Thriving* (Chicago: University of Chicago Press, 1998); Robert Woodberry and Christian Smith, "Fundamentalism et al: Conservative Protestants in America," *Annual Review of Sociology* 24, no. 1 (1998): 25–56.

6. See Christopher P. Scheitle, David R. Johnson, and Elaine Howard Ecklund, "Scientists and Religious Leaders Compete for Cultural Authority of Science," *Public Understanding of Science* 27, no. 1 (2018): 57–75.

7. See recent studies from Pew Research Center: "Religion and Science," Pew Research Center, October 22, 2015, https://www.pewresearch.org/science/2015/10/22/science-and-religion; Cary Funk and David Masci, "5 Facts about the Interplay between Religion and Science," October 22, 2015, https://www.pewresearch.org/fact-tank/2015/10/22/5-facts-about-the-interplay-between-religion-and-science.

8. Over the years I have developed a research habit of naming studies according to initials. Each person I interview for a study receives a "respondent code" consisting of the study initials and a number. Making sure that I attach the code to any respondent quotation allows me to make sure I am not over-quoting the same respondent and to quickly find the demographic information for a specific respondent, as well as to de-identify data. (I start calling most respondents by their code rather than by their names, although I do give pseudonyms to some respondents, and all respondent names in this book are pseudonyms.) The specific studies that I refer to in this book are the Real Change study (RC), an interview-based study of Christians in science; the Religion among Scientists in International Context study (RASIC), an eight-nation study of scientists' attitudes toward religion; the Religious Understandings of Science study (RUS), a US-based study examining how religious people view science and scientists; and Religion, Inequality, and Science Education (RISE), an interview-based study in Houston about how Hispanic, Black, and Korean Christians view race, equality, and science.

9. Robert T. Pennock, "The Scientific Virtues Project," Michigan State University, 2019, https://msu.edu/~pennock5/research/SVP.html; see also "Character Traits: Scientific Virtue," *Nature* 532, no. 7597 (April 2016): 139, DOI:10.1038/nj7597-139a.

Chapter 2 Overlapping Communities

1. RC_05, Plasma Physics, Research Professor, Male, Evangelical, conducted March 7, 2018. James was interviewed as part of the Real Change study (RC), a study of how scientists who are Christians understand the relationship between their faith and their scientific work.

2. See Elaine Howard Ecklund and Christopher P. Scheitle, *Religion vs. Science: What Religious People Really Think* (New York: Oxford University Press, 2017), 65.

3. RASIC_US03, Biology, Graduate Student, Female, conducted March 2, 2015. This subject was interviewed as part of the Religion among Scientists in International Context study (RASIC).

4. RC_10, Physics, Professor, Female, Evangelical, conducted March 29, 2018.

5. RC_07, Genetics, Associate Professor, Male, Evangelical, conducted March 9, 2018.

6. RC_03, Biology, Associate Professor, Male, Evangelical Covenant, conducted February 19, 2018.

7. See, e.g., Christopher P. Scheitle and Elaine Howard Ecklund, "Perceptions of Religious Discrimination among U.S. Scientists," *Journal for the Scientific Study of Religion* 57, no. 1 (2018): 139–55.

8. See Elaine Howard Ecklund, David R. Johnson, Brandon Vaidyanathan, Kirstin R. W. Matthews, Steven W. Lewis, Robert A. Thomson Jr., and Di Di, *Secularity and Science: What Scientists around the World Really Think about Religion* (New York: Oxford University Press, 2019).

9. Scheitle and Ecklund, "Perceptions of Religious Discrimination," 153.

10. RC_09, Biology, Professor and Department Chair, Male, Christian Reformed Church, conducted March 22, 2018.

11. RC_10, Physics, Professor, Female, Evangelical, conducted March 29, 2018.

12. RC_08, Evolutionary Biology and Climate Change, Research Faculty, Female, Christian Reformed Church, conducted March 21, 2018.

13. Gordon Gauchat, "Politicization of Science in the Public Sphere: A Study of Public Trust in the United States, 1974–2010," *American Sociological Review* 77, no. 2 (2012): 167–87.

14. RC_05, Plasma Physics, Research Professor, Male, Evangelical, conducted March 7, 2018.

15. RC_07, Genetics, Associate Professor, Male, Evangelical, conducted March 9, 2018, his emphasis.

16. RUS_Mid-High/High SES Evangelical Church Houston Int5, conducted July 5, 2011. This subject was interviewed as part of the Religious Understandings of Science study (RUS).

17. This data is from the Religious Understandings of Science study (2013–14). According to this same study, by comparison, 17 percent of those who identify as nonreligious place hardly any confidence in colleges or universities.

18. RC_08, Evolutionary Biology and Climate Change, Research Faculty, Female, Christian Reformed Church, conducted March 21, 2018.

19. RC_10, Physics, Professor, Female, Evangelical, conducted March 29, 2018.

20. RC_09, Biology, Professor and Department Chair, Male, Christian Reformed Church, conducted March 22, 2018.

21. RC_06, Immunology and Rheumatology, Associate Professor, Male, Evangelical, conducted March 8, 2018.

22. RC_02, Evolutionary Biology, Associate Professor, Female, Christian, conducted February 14, 2018.

23. RC_01, Physical Chemistry, Professor, Female, Baptist, conducted February 14, 2018.

24. RC_06, Immunology and Rheumatology, Associate Professor, Male, Evangelical Christian, conducted March 8, 2018.

25. RC_09, Biology, Professor and Department Chair, Male, Christian Reformed Church, conducted March 22, 2018.

26. The statistics in this paragraph are based on analyses from the Religious Understandings of Science (RUS) study.

27. RC_06, Immunology and Rheumatology, Associate Professor, Male, Evangelical Christian, conducted March 8, 2018.

28. RC_09, Biology, Professor and Department Chair, Male, Christian Reformed Church, conducted March 22, 2018.

29. RC_04, Genetics, Professor, Female, Christian, conducted March 4, 2018.

30. RUS_High SES Evangelical Church Houston Int5, conducted July 22, 2012.

31. See, e.g., "Character Traits: Scientific Virtue," *Nature* 532, no. 7597 (April 2016): 139, DOI:10.1038/nj7597-139a.

32. Scotty Hendricks, "You Morally Elevate People Like Yourself, Study Finds," Big Think, August 31, 2018, https://bigthink.com/scotty-hendricks/the-mere-liking-effect-why-you-trust-people-who-are-like-you.

33. Michael Siegrist, George T. Cvetkovich, and Heinz Gutscher, "Shared Values, Social Trust, and the Perception of Geographic Cancer Clusters," *Risk Analysis* 21, no. 6 (2001): 1047–54.

34. See the many resources from Greg Cootsona and Drew Rick Miller's new program Science for the Church, at https://scienceforthechurch.org.

35. RC_09, Biology, Professor and Department Chair, Male, Christian Reformed Church, conducted March 22, 2018.

36. RC_08, Evolutionary Biology and Climate Change, Research Faculty, Female, Christian Reformed Church, conducted March 21, 2018.

37. RC_06, Immunology and Rheumatology, Associate Professor, Male, Evangelical Christian, conducted March 8, 2018.

38. Tom McLeish, "Thinking Differently about Science and Religion," *Physics Today*, February 2018, 10–12.

Chapter 3 Creative Evolution: Moving Past the Origins Debate

1. Religion among Scientists in International Context (RASIC) study (2013–15).

2. Religious Understandings of Science (RUS) study (2013–14).

3. See Elaine Howard Ecklund and Christopher P. Scheitle, *Religion vs. Science: What Religious People Really Think* (New York: Oxford University Press, 2017), 77.

4. See Ecklund and Scheitle, *Religion vs. Science*, 77.

5. RUS_Mid-High SES Black Protestant Church Houston Int3, conducted August 8, 2012.

6. See Ecklund and Scheitle, *Religion vs. Science*, 78.

7. Esther Chan and Elaine Howard Ecklund, "Narrating and Navigating Authorities: Evangelical and Mainline Protestant Interpretations of the Bible and Science," *Journal for the Scientific Study of Religion* 55, no. 1 (2016): 54–69.

8. RUS_High SES Evangelical Church Houston Int18, conducted May 29, 2012.

9. RUS_High SES Evangelical Church Houston Int23, conducted June 21, 2012.

10. RUS_Low SES Evangelical Church Houston Int2, conducted August 18, 2013.

11. RUS_Low SES Black Protestant Church Chicago Int15, conducted November 10, 2013.

12. Francis Collins, *The Language of God: A Scientist Presents Evidence for Belief* (New York: Free Press, 2007), 140–41.

13. Ryan Bebej, "From Young-Earth Creationist to Whale Evolution Expert: My Story," BioLogos, February 6, 2018, https://biologos.org/blogs/guest/from-young-earth-creationist-to-whale-evolution-expert-my-story.

14. RC_02, Evolutionary Biology, Associate Professor, Female, Christian, conducted February 14, 2018.

15. See Ecklund and Scheitle, *Religion vs. Science*, 72.

16. RUS_High SES Evangelical Church Houston Int9, conducted February 13, 2013.

17. See Ecklund and Scheitle, *Religion vs. Science*, 73.

18. RC_10, Physics, Professor, Female, Evangelical Christian, conducted March 29, 2018.

19. See Ecklund and Scheitle, *Religion vs. Science*, 80.

20. RUS_High SES Mainline Church Houston Int16, conducted June 20, 2012.

21. RUS_High SES Mainline Church Houston Int5, conducted September 2, 2011.

22. Richard N. Ostling, "The Search for the Historical Adam," *Christianity Today*, June 3, 2011, 24.

23. RUS_High SES Evangelical Church Chicago Int5, conducted July 18, 2013.

24. RC_07, Genetics, Associate Professor, Male, Evangelical, conducted March 9, 2018.

25. RUS_Low SES Evangelical Church Houston Int5, conducted September 13, 2013.

26. RC_01, Physical Chemistry, Professor, Female, Baptist, conducted February 14, 2018.

27. See Greg Cootsona, *Mere Science and Christian Faith: Bridging the Divide with Emerging Adults* (Downers Grove, IL: InterVarsity, 2018), 93.

28. RUS_Low SES Black Protestant Church Chicago Int15, conducted November 10, 2013.

29. RUS_High SES Evangelical Church Houston Int25, conducted July 8, 2013.

30. RUS_High SES Evangelical Church Chicago Int2, conducted July 16, 2013.

31. David Unander, "Race: A Brief History of Its Origin, Failure and Alternative," BioLogos, February 21, 2018, https://biologos.org/blogs/guest/race-a-brief-history-of-its-origin-failure-and-alternative.

32. See W. James Booth, "Communities of Memory: On Identity, Memory, and Debt," *American Political Science Review* 93, no. 2 (1999): 249.

33. RUS_Low SES Black Protestant Church Houston Int19, conducted August 11, 2011.

34. RUS_Low SES Black Protestant Church Houston Int17_RL, conducted August 9, 2011.

35. RUS_Low SES Black Protestant Church Houston Int17_RL, conducted August 9, 2011.

36. Mario Livio, *Why? What Makes Us Curious* (New York: Simon & Schuster, 2017), 133.

Chapter 4 Curiosity

1. RAAS_Chem18, conducted January 30, 2006. "Jill" is not her real name; to protect her identity some details have been obscured. I mention this respondent in my book *Science vs. Religion*, but there I focus on different pieces of her narrative. See Elaine Howard Ecklund, *Science vs. Religion: What Scientists Really Think* (New York: Oxford University Press, 2010). The Religion among Academic Scientists study (RAAS) is a broad study of "religion, spirituality, and ethics among university scientists at twenty-one elite research universities in the United States." Ecklund, *Science vs. Religion*, 157.

2. Elias Baumgarten, "Curiosity as a Moral Virtue," *International Journal of Applied Philosophy* 15, no. 2 (2001): 169.

3. See Stanley Fish, "Does Curiosity Kill More Than the Cat?," opinion, *New York Times*, September 14, 2009, https://opinionator.blogs.nytimes.com//2009/09/14/does-curiosity-kill-more-than-the-cat.

4. Marcel Schwantes, "This Famous Albert Einstein Quote Nails It: The Smartest People Today Display This 1 Trait," Inc., February 15, 2018, https://www.inc.com/marcel-schwantes/this-1-simple-way-of-thinking-separates-smartest-people-from-everyone-else.html.

5. Mario Livio, *Why? What Makes Us Curious* (New York: Simon & Schuster, 2017), 141.

6. This excerpt is from an interview by Summer Ash with *Smithsonian Magazine*. Find it here: "Why Theoretical Physicist Sylvester James Gates Sees No Conflict between Science and Religion," Smithsonian.com, November 15, 2016, https://www.smithsonianmag.com/science-nature/why-theoretical-physicist-sylvester-james-gates-sees-no-conflict-between-science-and-religion-180961090/#ZXx5OkQAbIHz40yF.99.

7. Greg Cootsona, *Mere Science and Christian Faith: Bridging the Divide with Emerging Adults* (Downers Grove, IL: InterVarsity, 2018), 8. Cootsona also writes in his book, "We as Christians believe Jesus is Lord of all. Therefore whatever any form of knowledge discovers [that is actually true]—anything in the sciences that is true—we are bound to bring these discoveries under the Lordship of Christ" (47).

8. Mario Livio, "The 'Why' behind Asking Why: The Science of Curiosity," Wharton School, University of Pennsylvania, August 23, 2017, https://knowledge.wharton.upenn.edu/article/makes-us-curious.

9. Mario Livio, "Why Curiosity Can Be Both Painful and Pleasurable," *Nautilus*, September 28, 2017, http://nautil.us/issue/52/the-hive/why-curiosity-can-be-both-painful-and-pleasurable.

Chapter 5 Doubt

1. See, in particular, Robert K. Merton, "The Normative Structure of Science," in *The Sociology of Science: Theoretical and Empirical Investigations*, ed. R. K. Merton (1942; repr., Chicago, IL: University of Chicago Press, 1973), 267–80.

2. I love this piece by Vance Morgan on doubt, in which Morgan discusses his perspective on the "doubting Thomas" story: Vance Morgan, "Why Doubt Is My Favorite Virtue," Patheos, *Freelance Christianity* (blog), April 27, 2019, https://www.patheos.com/blogs/freelancechristianity/why-doubt-is-my-favorite-virtue.

3. RUS_Low/Mid-Low SES Houston Female Evangelical Church Int7, conducted September 7, 2013.

4. See Peter Berger and Anton Zijderveld, *In Praise of Doubt: How to Have Convictions without Becoming a Fanatic* (New York: HarperOne, 2009), 10–11.

5. Though not about doubt per se, Daniel Migliore's classic touches on very relevant themes. See Daniel Migliore, *Faith Seeking Understanding: An Introduction to Christian Theology*, 3rd ed. (Grand Rapids: Eerdmans, 2014).

6. RUS_Mid-High/High SES Houston Female Evangelical Church Int6, conducted July 14, 2011.

7. RUS_Mid-High SES Chicago Male Evangelical Church Int9, conducted June 23, 2012.

8. These statistics come from the Religious Understandings of Science study.

9. These statistics come from the US survey in the RASIC study.

10. RC_03, Biology, Associate Professor, Male, Evangelical Covenant, conducted February 19, 2018.

11. RC_04, Genetics, Professor, Female, Christian, conducted March 4, 2018.

12. RUS_Mid-High SES Houston Female Evangelical Church Int18, conducted May 29, 2012.

13. RC_07, Genetics, Associate Professor, Male, Evangelical Christian, conducted May 9, 2018.

14. RC_08, Evolutionary Biology and Climate Change, Research Faculty, Female, Christian Reformed Church, conducted March 21, 2018.

15. Anne Lamott, *Almost Everything: Notes on Hope* (London: Penguin, 2018), 131.

Chapter 6 Humility

1. "Character Traits: Scientific Virtue," *Nature* 532, no. 7597 (April 2016): 139, DOI:10.1038/nj7597-139a.

2. Helen Dukas and Banesh Hoffman, eds., *Albert Einstein, the Human Side: Glimpses from His Archives* (Princeton: Princeton University Press, 2013), 48.

3. "Character Virtue Development: Intellectual Humility," John Templeton Foundation, 2019, https://www.templeton.org/discoveries/intellectual-humility.

4. Quoted in Allen Hammond, ed., *A Passion to Know: 20 Profiles in Science* (New York: Scribner, 1984), 5.

5. Connor Wood, "Science and Humility," Patheos, *Science on Religion* (blog), July 20, 2013, https://www.patheos.com/blogs/scienceonreligion/2013/07/science-and-humility.

6. *New World Encyclopedia*, s.v. "Johannes Kepler," last modified May 12, 2018, http://www.newworldencyclopedia.org/entry/Johannes_Kepler.

7. RC_05, Plasma Physics, Research Professor, Male, Evangelical, conducted March 7, 2018, his emphasis.

8. RC_08, Evolutionary Biology and Climate Change, Research Faculty, Female, Christian Reformed Church, conducted March 21, 2018.

9. RASIC_UK08, Biology, Professor, Male, conducted December 2, 2013.

10. RC_03, Computational Biology, Associate Professor, Male, Evangelical Covenant, conducted February 19, 2018.

11. Data comes from the Religious Understandings of Science study.

12. Amanda King, "Humility in Science: Because Science Always Wins," In-Training, July 6, 2016, http://in-training.org/humility-science-science-always-wins-11239.

13. Elaine Howard Ecklund, *Science vs. Religion: What Scientists Really Think* (New York: Oxford University Press, 2010), 38.

14. RC_03, Biology, Associate Professor, Male, Evangelical Covenant, conducted February 19, 2018.

15. RAAS_PS 4, conducted June 21, 2005. See Ecklund, *Science vs. Religion*, 39.

16. RAAS_Bio 9, conducted July 25, 2005.

17. RC_08, Evolutionary Biology and Climate Change, Research Faculty, Female, Christian Reformed Church, conducted March 21, 2018.

18. Elaine Howard Ecklund and Christopher P. Scheitle, *Religion vs. Science: What Religious People Really Think* (New York: Oxford University Press, 2017), 25.

19. Ecklund and Scheitle, *Religion vs. Science*, 27.

20. Data is from my Religious Understandings of Science study, conducted 2014–16.

21. RC_06, Immunology and Rheumatology, Associate Professor, Male, Evangelical Christian, conducted March 8, 2018.

22. Data is from my Religious Understandings of Science study.

23. RC_06, Immunology and Rheumatology, Associate Professor, Male, Evangelical Christian, conducted March 8, 2018.

24. RC_10, Physics, Professor, Female, Evangelical Christian, conducted March 29, 2018.

25. RC_05, Plasma Physics, Research Professor, Male, Evangelical, conducted March 7, 2018.

26. RC_03, Biology, Associate Professor, Male, Evangelical Covenant, conducted February 19, 2018.

27. RC_06, Immunology and Rheumatology, Associate Professor, Male, Evangelical Christian, conducted March 8, 2018.

Chapter 7 Creativity

1. RC_10, Physics, Professor, Female, Evangelical, conducted March 29, 2018.

2. Scott Barry Kaufman, "The Philosophy of Creativity," *Scientific American*, *Beautiful Minds* (blog), May 12, 2014, https://blogs.scientificamerican.com/beautiful-minds/the-philosophy-of-creativity/?redirect=1.

3. Dorothy Sayers, *The Mind of the Maker* (New York: HarperSanFrancisco, 1941), 17.

4. Robert Gilbert, *Science and the Truthfulness of Beauty: How the Personal Perspective Discovers Creation* (Abingdon, UK: Routledge, 2018), 64.

5. RC_02, Evolutionary Biology, Associate Professor, Female, Christian, conducted February 14, 2018.

6. Michael Taylor, "Glorifying God with Infertility," GoThereFor.com, April 13, 2017, http://gotherefor.com/offer.php?intid=29614&changestore=true.

7. Jeff Cavanaugh, "How the Church Makes the Trial of Infertility Better (or Worse)," The Gospel Coalition, December 25, 2013, https://www.thegospelcoalition.org/article/how-the-church-makes-the-trial-of-infertility-better-or-worse.

8. Philip Wheeler, "A Silent Grief: Pastoral Reflections on Infertility," Mattiasmedia.com, September 27, 2000, http://matthiasmedia.com/briefing/2000/09/a-silent-grief-pastoral-reflections-on-infertility.

9. Wheeler, "Silent Grief."

10. Megan Best, "Your Options in Infertility," The Gospel Coalition, March 19, 2014, https://www.thegospelcoalition.org/article/your-options-in-infertility.

11. Elizabeth Hagan, "5 Ways the Church Could Show More Compassion for Those Struggling with Infertility," *Time*, May 22, 2017, http://time.com/4786683/church-views-infertility.

12. "Assisted Reproductive Technology," Medline Plus, May 14, 2018, https://medlineplus.gov/assistedreproductivetechnology.html.

13. Jennifer Gerson Uffalussy, "The Cost of IVF: 4 Things I Learned While Battling Infertility," *Forbes*, February 6, 2014, https://www.forbes.com/sites/learnvest/2014/02/06/the-cost-of-ivf-4-things-i-learned-while-battling-infertility/#21770c0924dd.

14. "IVF by the Numbers," Penn Medicine, *Fertility Blog*, March 14, 2018, https://www.pennmedicine.org/updates/blogs/fertility-blog/2018/march/ivf-by-the-numbers.

15. Ariana Eunjung Cha, "How Religion Is Coming to Terms with Modern Fertility Methods," *Washington Post*, April 27, 2018, https://www.washingtonpost.com/graphics/2018/national/how-religion-is-coming-to-terms-with-modern-fertility-methods/?utm_term=.19f2a08c8634.

16. Elaine Howard Ecklund and Christopher P. Scheitle, *Religion vs. Science: What Religious People Really Think* (New York: Oxford University Press, 2017), 128.

17. RUS_Low/Mid-Low SES Evangelical Church Houston Int10, conducted November 13, 2013.

18. Taylor, "Glorifying God with Infertility."

19. Data from Religious Understandings of Science (RUS) study.

20. RUS_Mid-High/High SES Evangelical Church Houston Int15, conducted October 2, 2013.

21. RUS_Low SES Evangelical Church Houston Int9, conducted October 1, 2013.

22. RC_09, Biology, Professor, Male, Christian Reformed Church, conducted March 22, 2018.

23. Cary Funk, Brian Kennedy, and Elizabeth Podrebarac Sciupac, "U.S. Public Wary of Biomedical Technologies to 'Enhance' Human Abilities," Pew Research

Center, July 26, 2016, updated November 2, 2016, http://www.pewinternet.org/2016/07/26/u-s-public-wary-of-biomedical-technologies-to-enhance-human-abilities, see page 7 under "2. U.S. public opinion on the future use of gene editing."

24. Funk, Kennedy, and Podrebarac Sciupac, "U.S. Public Wary," http://www.pewinternet.org/2016/07/26/u-s-public-wary-of-biomedical-technologies-to-enhance-human-abilities, see page 7 under "Uncertainty, Divisions over Moral Acceptability of Gene Editing."

25. Funk, Kennedy, and Podrebarac Sciupac, "U.S. Public Wary," http://www.pewinternet.org/2016/07/26/u-s-public-wary-of-biomedical-technologies-to-enhance-human-abilities, see page 8, table titled "White Evangelicals Especially Likely to Say Gene Editing for Babies Crosses a Line; Most Atheists and Agnostics Say It Is Just Another Avenue to Betterment."

26. RUS_High SES Evangelical Church Chicago Int8, conducted July 20, 2013.

27. RUS_Low SES African American Evangelical Church Int18, conducted August 10, 2011.

28. RUS_Mid-High/High SES Evangelical Church Houston Int15, conducted December 10, 2011.

29. National Academies of Sciences, Engineering, and Medicine, *Human Genome Editing: Science, Ethics, and Governance* (Washington, DC: The National Academies Press, 2017).

30. RUS_Mid-High/High SES Evangelical Church Houston Int5, conducted July 5, 2011.

Chapter 8 Healing

1. RC_09, Biology, Professor, Male, Christian Reformed Church, conducted March 22, 2018

2. RC_06, Computational Biology, Associate Professor, Male, Evangelical Covenant, conducted February 19, 2018.

3. RC_09, Biology, Professor, Male, Christian Reformed Church, conducted March 22, 2018.

4. See Elaine Howard Ecklund and Christopher P. Scheitle, *Religion vs. Science: What Religious People Really Think* (New York: Oxford University Press, 2017), 130.

5. RUS_Mid-Low SES Missionary Baptist Church Chicago Int3, conducted July 18, 2013.

6. RUS_Low/Mid-Low SES Evangelical Christian Church Houston Int9, conducted October 1, 2013.

7. RC_09, Biology, Professor and Department Chair, Male, Christian Reformed Church, conducted March 22, 2018.

8. Ecklund and Scheitle, *Religion vs. Science*, 117.

9. John H. Evans, *Playing God? Human Genetic Engineering and the Rationalization of Public Bioethical Debate* (Chicago: University of Chicago Press, 2002); see also Courtney S. Campbell, "The Ordeal and Meaning of Suffering," *Sunstone* 18, no. 3 (1995): 37–43.

10. Ecklund and Scheitle, *Religion vs. Science*, 129.

11. John H. Evans, "The Road to Enhancement, via Human Gene Editing, Is Paved with Good Intentions," *The Conversation*, November 27, 2018, http://theconversation.com/the-road-to-enhancement-via-human-gene-editing-is-paved-with-good-intentions-107677.

12. Junying Yu and James A. Thomson, "Embryonic Stem Cells," National Institutes of Health, 2016, https://stemcells.nih.gov/info/Regenerative_Medicine/2006 Chapter1.htm.

13. Yu and Thomson, "Embryonic Stem Cells."

14. "Embryonic Stem Cell Research: An Ethical Dilemma," EuroStemCell, 2019, https://www.eurostemcell.org/embryonic-stem-cell-research-ethical-dilemma.

15. Ecklund and Scheitle, *Religion vs. Science*, 121.

16. Religion among Scientists in International Context (RASIC), 2011–15.

17. RUS_High SES Mainline Church Houston Int25, conducted June 21, 2013.

18. RISE_AAB03, Accountant, Female, conducted January 22, 2016. The Religion, Inequality, and Science Education (RISE) study is interviews of black, Latino/a, and Korean Christians about their attitudes toward science and medicine.

19. RC_07, Genetics, Associate Professor, Male, Evangelical, conducted March 9, 2018.

20. RC_03, Computational Biology, Associate Professor, Male, Evangelical Covenant, conducted February 19, 2018.

21. Tomislav Mestrovic, "CRISPR: Ethical and Safety Concerns," News-Medical .Net, August 23, 2018, https://www.news-medical.net/life-sciences/CRISPR-Ethical -and-Safety-Concerns.aspx.

22. PedsOnc5, conducted October 19, 2005. As part of the broader Religion among Academic Scientists study, I conducted interviews with professors of pediatrics and pediatric oncology at medical schools. Some of this work has been published elsewhere. See, e.g., Wendy Cadge, Elaine Howard Ecklund, and Nicholas Short, "Constructions of Religion and Spirituality in the Daily Boundary Work of Pediatric Physicians," *Social Problems* 56, no. 4 (2009): 702–21.

23. David Zuleger, "God Brings Us Suffering for Others' Sake," *Desiring God*, July 6, 2015, https://www.desiringgod.org/articles/god-brings-us-suffering-for-others-sake.

24. Sue Bohlin, "The Value of Suffering: A Christian Perspective," Probe Ministries *Probe for Answers* (blog), May 27, 2000, https://probe.org/the-value-of-suffering.

25. RC_09, Biology, Professor, Male, Christian Reformed Church, conducted March 22, 2018.

26. Todd Neva, "The Purpose of Suffering," *Neva Story* (blog), March 14, 2017, http://nevastory.com/the-purpose-of-suffering.

27. Todd Neva, "Did He Allow It? A Response to a Question after the Father's Day Flash Floods in the Keweenaw," *Neva Story* (blog), June 19, 2018, http://nevastory .com/did-he-allow-it.

28. See Kate Bowler, *Everything Happens for a Reason: And Other Lies I've Loved* (New York: Random House, 2018), 123, 121. See also Kate Bowler, "'Everything Happens for a Reason'—and Other Lies I've Loved," filmed December 2018, TedMed, 14:43, https://www.ted.com/talks/kate_bowler_everything_happens_for_a_reason_and _other_lies_i_ve_loved?.

29. "Core Values and History," ECHO, https://www.echonet.org/core-values-history.

30. RC_03, Computational Biology, Associate Professor, Male, Evangelical Covenant, conducted February 19, 2018.

Chapter 9 Awe

1. Learn more about Jennifer Wiseman here: "Dr. Jennifer J. Wiseman—Hubble Senior Project Scientist," NASA, August 3, 2017, https://www.nasa.gov/content/goddard /dr-jennifer-j-wiseman-hubble-senior-project-scientist.

2. Richard P. Feynman, *What Do You Care What Other People Think? Further Adventures of a Curious Character* (New York: Norton, 1988), 11.

3. Richard Dawkins, *Unweaving the Rainbow: Science, Delusion, and the Appetite for Wonder* (Boston: Mariner, 2000), x.

4. Walter Isaacson, *Einstein: His Life and Universe* (New York: Simon & Schuster, 2007), 548.

5. Paul Piff and Dacher Keltner, "Why Do We Experience Awe?," *New York Times*, opinion, May 22, 2015, https://www.nytimes.com/2015/05/24/opinion/sunday/why-do-we-experience-awe.html.

6. Kristján Kristjánsson, *Virtuous Emotions* (New York: Oxford University Press, 2018), 144–45.

7. RASIC_US64, Physics, Graduate Student, Male, conducted April 17, 2015.

8. RC_08, Evolutionary Biology and Climate Change, Research Faculty, Female, Christian Reformed Church, conducted March 21, 2018.

9. RC_09, Biology, Professor and Department Chair, Male, Christian Reformed Church, conducted March 22, 2018.

10. RC_03, Biology, Associate Professor, Male, Evangelical Covenant, conducted February 19, 2018; see also Andrew Wilson, *Spirit and Sacrament: An Invitation to Eucharismatic Worship* (Grand Rapids: Zondervan, 2018), who has similar sentiments.

11. RC_07, Genetics, Associate Professor, Male, Evangelical Christian, conducted March 9, 2018.

12. RASIC_US49, Physics, Graduate Student, Female, conducted April 8, 2015.

13. RC_08, Evolutionary Biology and Climate Change, Research Faculty, Female, Christian Reformed Church, conducted March 21, 2018.

14. RC_03, Biology, Associate Professor, Male, Evangelical Covenant, conducted February 19, 2018.

15. RASIC_US61, Physics, Graduate Student, Female, conducted April 15, 2015.

16. RASIC_US67, Biology, Graduate Student, Female, conducted April 21, 2015.

17. RASIC_US60, Biology, Associate Professor, Female, conducted April 15, 2015.

18. RASIC_US11, Physics, Professor, Female, conducted March 25, 2015.

19. Elaine Howard Ecklund and Elizabeth Long, "Scientists and Spirituality," *Sociology of Religion* 72, no. 3 (2011): 266.

20. Elaine Howard Ecklund and Christopher P. Scheitle, *Religion vs. Science: What Religious People Really Think* (New York: Oxford University Press, 2017), 22.

21. Ecklund and Scheitle, *Religion vs. Science*, 20.

22. Ecklund and Scheitle, *Religion vs. Science*, 21.

23. Sandra Knispel, "Does Awe Lead to Greater Interest in Science?," University of Rochester Newscenter, March 6, 2019, https://www.rochester.edu/newscenter/does-awe-lead-to-greater-interest-in-science-366192.

24. Paul David Tripp, *Awe: Why It Matters for Everything We Think, Say, and Do* (Wheaton: Crossway, 2015), 18.

Chapter 10 Shalom

1. Josie Lacey, "The Ideal of Peace in Judaism," Israel and Judaism Studies, 2006, https://www.ijs.org.au/the-ideal-of-peace-in-judaism.

2. Walter Brueggemann, *The Prophetic Imagination*, 2nd ed. (Minneapolis: Fortress, 2001), 88.

3. "Tikkun Olam: Repairing the World," My Jewish Learning, 2018, https://www.myjewishlearning.com/article/tikkun-olam-repairing-the-world.

4. RUS_High SES Reform Jewish Synagogue Chicago Int18, conducted July 17, 2013.

5. RASIC_IND36, Biology, Assistant Professor, Male, conducted May 23, 2014.

6. RASIC_IND53, Physics, Senior Professor, Male, conducted May 26, 2014.

7. RC_08, Evolutionary Biology and Climate Change, Research Faculty, Female, Christian Reformed Church, conducted March 21, 2018.

8. RC_08, Evolutionary Biology and Climate Change, Research Faculty, Female, Christian Reformed Church, conducted March 21, 2018.

9. See Tommy Grimm, "When I Run, I Feel God's Pleasure," *The Connection* (blog), August 10, 2012, https://sites.duke.edu/theconnection/2012/08/10/exercising-for-joy. See also *Chariots of Fire*, directed by Hugh Hudson, written by Colin Welland (London: Goldcrest Films, 1981), DVD.

10. RC_02, Evolutionary Biology, Associate Professor, Female, Christian, conducted February 14, 2018.

11. RC_06, Immunology and Rheumatology, Associate Professor, Male, Evangelical, conducted March 8, 2018.

12. RC_03, Biology, Associate Professor, Male, Evangelical Covenant, conducted February 19, 2018.

13. Elaine Howard Ecklund and Christopher P. Scheitle, *Religion vs. Science: What Religious People Really Think* (New York: Oxford University Press, 2017), 95. While this number seems large, I found that 13.4 percent of all respondents described themselves as "not at all interested," only slightly lower and statistically equivalent.

14. RUS_Mid-High/High SES Evangelical Church Houston Int4, conducted June 22, 2011.

15. Ann Neumann, "Katharine Hayhoe: God's Creation Is Running a Fever," *Guernica*, December 15, 2014, https://www.guernicamag.com/gods-creation-is-running-a-fever.

16. Dorothy F. Chappell, "Worshipping God through Discovery and Science," in *When God and Science Meet: Surprising Discoveries of Agreement* (Washington, DC: National Association of Evangelicals, 2015), 38.

17. RUS_High SES Evangelical Church Chicago Int8, conducted June 22, 2012.

18. RASIC_UK64, Physics, Graduate Student, Male, conducted April 17, 2015.

19. RUS_High SES Evangelical Church Houston Int13, conducted August 31, 2012.

20. RUS_High SES Mainline Church Houston Int1, conducted July 14, 2011.

21. RC_02, Evolutionary Biology, Associate Professor, Female, Christian, conducted February 14, 2018.

22. David Masci, Besheer Mohamed, and Gregory A. Smith, "Black Americans Are More Likely Than Overall Public to Be Christian, Protestant," Pew Research Center, April 23, 2018, https://www.pewresearch.org/fact-tank/2018/04/23/black-americans-are-more-likely-than-overall-public-to-be-christian-protestant.

23. RC_04, Genetics, Professor, Female, Christian, conducted March 4, 2018.

24. RISE_AfAm41, African American, Pastor, Male, conducted September 29, 2015.

25. RISE_Lat23, Latino, Pastor, Male, conducted September 14, 2015.

26. RC_09, Biology, Professor and Department Chair, Male, Christian Reformed Church, conducted March 22, 2018.

27. RC_03, Biology, Associate Professor, Male, Evangelical Covenant, conducted February 19, 2018.

28. RC_03, Biology, Associate Professor, Male, Evangelical Covenant, conducted February 19, 2018.

Chapter 11 Gratitude

1. Kirtan Nautiyal, "We Are Scientists," LongReads, June 4, 2018, https://longreads.com/2018/06/04/we-are-scientists.

2. Elaine Howard Ecklund and Christopher P. Scheitle, *Religion vs. Science: What Religious People Really Think* (New York: Oxford University Press, 2017), 23.

3. Emma Green, "Gratitude without God," *The Atlantic*, November 26, 2014, https://www.theatlantic.com/health/archive/2014/11/the-phenomenology-of-gratitude/383174; see also Robert Emmons, "The Psychology of Gratitude: Robert Emmons on How Saying Thanks Makes You Happier," November 19, 2018, in *The Table Podcast*, produced by Biola University Center for Christian Thought, MP3 audio, 28:05, https://cct.biola.edu/psychology-gratitude-robert-emmons-saying-thanks-makes-happier.

4. John S. Knox, "King David," Ancient History Encyclopedia, October 18, 2017, https://www.ancient.eu/King_David.

5. Quoted in Robert A. Emmons and Michael E. McCullough, *The Psychology of Gratitude* (Oxford: Oxford University Press, 2004), 123.

6. Paul J. Mills, Laura Redwine, Kathleen Wilson, Meredith A. Pung, et al., "The Role of Gratitude in Spiritual Well-Being in Asymptomatic Heart Failure Patients," *Spiritual Clinical Practices* 2, no. 1 (2015): 5–17.

7. Lauren Dunn, "Be Thankful: Science Says Gratitude Is Good for Your Health," Today.com, November 26, 2015, last updated May 12, 2017, https://www.today.com/health/be-thankful-science-says-gratitude-good-your-health-t58256; see also Sunghyon Kyeong, Joohan Kim, Dae Jin Kim, Hesun Erin Kim, and Jae-Jin Kim, "Effects of Gratitude Meditation on Neural Network Functional Connectivity and Brain-Heart Coupling," *Scientific Reports* 7 (2017), https://www.nature.com/articles/s41598-017-05520-9.

8. Summer Allen, "The Science of Gratitude: A White Paper Prepared for the John Templeton Foundation by the Greater Good Science Center at UC Berkeley," Greater Good Science Center at UC Berkeley, May 2018, https://ggsc.berkeley.edu/images/uploads/GGSC-JTF_White_Paper-Gratitude-FINAL.pdf.

9. Chih-Che Lin, "A Higher-Order Gratitude Uniquely Predicts Subjective Well-Being: Incremental Validity above the Personality and a Single Gratitude," *Indicators Research* 119, no. 2 (2013): 909–24.

10. Allen, "Science of Gratitude," 4.

11. See, e.g., Ecklund and Scheitle, *Religion vs. Science*; see also Kristin Layous, Kate Sweeny, Christina Armenta, Soojung Na, Incheol Choi, and Sonja Lyubomirsky, "The Proximal Experience of Gratitude," *PLOS One*, July 7, 2017, DOI: https://doi.org/10.1371/journal.pone.0179123.

12. RUS_Low SES African American Evangelical Church Houston Int19, conducted August 11, 2011.

13. See Diana Butler Bass, *Grateful: The Transformative Power of Giving Thanks* (San Francisco: HarperOne, 2018), n.p.

14. RC_04, Genetics, Professor, Female, Christian, conducted March 4, 2018.

15. RC_06, Immunology and Rheumatology, Associate Professor, Male, Evangelical, conducted March 8, 2018, his emphasis.

16. RC_02, Evolutionary Biology, Associate Professor, Female, Christian, conducted February 14, 2018, her emphasis.

17. RUS_Low SES African American Evangelical Church Houston Int19, conducted August 11, 2011.

18. RUS_Low SES Evangelical Church Houston Int2, conducted June 22, 2011.

19. RUS_High SES Evangelical Church Houston Int16, conducted October 25, 2012.

20. Ecklund and Scheitle, *Religion vs. Science,* 22.

21. RUS_Mid-High SES Evangelical Church Chicago Int1, conducted June 18, 2012.

22. RUS_High SES Mainline Church Chicago Int11, conducted July 21, 2013.

23. RC_05, Plasma Physics, Research Professor, Male, Evangelical, conducted March 7, 2018.

24. RC_06, Immunology and Rheumatology, Associate Professor, Male, Evangelical, conducted March 8, 2018.

25. Stephen Jay Gould, "Nonoverlapping Magisteria," The Unofficial Stephen Jay Gould Archive, http://www.stephenjaygould.org/library/gould_noma.html.

26. Elaine Howard Ecklund, *Science vs. Religion: What Scientists Really Think* (New York: Oxford University Press, 2010), 150.

27. Ecklund, *Science vs. Religion*, 137.

28. RAAS_Phys 34, conducted April 11, 2006.

29. RAAS_Bio 20, conducted January 24, 2006.

30. Ecklund, *Science vs. Religion*, 150.

31. Allen, "Science of Gratitude," 2–3, 15.